BROKEN BOUNDS

Winnicott Studies Monograph Series
Published and distributed by Karnac Books

Other titles in the series:

The Person Who Is Me: Contemporary Perspectives on the True and False Self
edited by Val Richards

Fathers, Families, and the Outside World
edited by Val Richards

André Green at The Squiggle Foundation
edited by Jan Abram

Art, Creativity, Living
edited by Lesley Caldwell

The Elusive Child
edited by Lesley Caldwell

Sex and Sexuality: Winnicottian Perspectives
edited by Lesley Caldwell

Winnicott and the Psychoanalytic Tradition: Interpretation and Other Psychoanalytic Issues
edited by Lesley Caldwell

The *Squiggle* Foundation is a registered charity set up in 1981 to study and cultivate the tradition of D. W. Winnicott. For further information, contact: The Administrator, Tel: 07534422117, email: info@squiggle-foundation.org

BROKEN BOUNDS
Contemporary Reflections on the Antisocial Tendency

Edited by
Christopher Reeves

Routledge
Taylor & Francis Group

LONDON AND NEW YORK

First published 2012 by Karnac Books Ltd.

Published 2018 by Routledge
2 Park Square, Milton Park, Abingdon, Oxon OX14 4RN
711 Third Avenue, New York, NY 10017, USA

Routledge is an imprint of the Taylor & Francis Group, an informa business

British Library Cataloguing in Publication Data

A C.I.P. for this book is available from the British Library

ISBN-13: 9781780490373 (pbk)

Typeset by Vikatan Publishing Solutions (P) Ltd., Chennai, India

In Memory of John Armstrong 1913–2011
Headmaster, the Mulberry Bush School 1964–1980

CONTENTS

PREFACE

In the course of these lectures, frequent reference is made to Donald Winnicott and his work, so it seems appropriate to offer a few introductory words about him. Winnicott was a paediatrician and psychoanalyst, who was born in 1896 in Plymouth and died in 1971 in London. In addition to his clinical practice with children and adults, he wrote many articles which were collected into books both during his lifetime and after. These range from theoretical and clinical papers intended primarily for an audience of fellow analysts (including the one on "The Antisocial Tendency", frequently referred to by the contributors to this volume), to lectures to a variety of professionals—social workers, health visitors, teachers, as well as doctors, members of the clergy, and groups of parents. In addition to his writing and lecturing, Winnicott was well known to the public in his lifetime owing to his radio broadcasts during World War II and after. Interest in his work continues to this day, promoted both by the Winnicott Trust, which has overseen the posthumous publication of most of his writings and the Squiggle Foundation, set up in 1981 through the energy and enterprise of a social worker, Alexander Newman, to provide lectures, seminars, and conferences promoting Winnicott's views about the centrality of the mother–infant relationship for the future well-being of the child and the importance of supporting that relationship on the part of the community, society, and government. The present collection of lectures is testimony to the continuance of this endeavour.

Much of course has changed in the field of communication since Winnicott's death forty years ago, not just in means, but in manner and style. Among many other aspects, greater attention is now given in the written and spoken word to the avoidance of gender stereotyping and of language use that might reflect such stereotyping. This obligation can pose a practical challenge for speakers especially (and, remember, the texts which follow were initially intended to be heard rather than read). The need to appear inclusive can occasionally militate against euphony and even comprehensibility. In consideration of this, it has been decided that from time to time in these texts the word "he" or "she" singly should be used in preference to "he/she" or "s/he" as a composite, even though reference to either or both sexes is implied by the context. To dispel any ambiguity on this score, of the various establishments for young people referred to in the course of these lectures, it should be stated that the Mulberry Bush School provides for infant and junior school aged children of both sexes; the Cotswold Community provides for boys only, aged from ten to sixteen; and Hillingcombe provides for girls and boys of a similar age range. In each of these establishments there are both male and female staff.

ABOUT THE EDITOR AND CONTRIBUTORS

Ann Horne is a retired Consultant Child and Adolescent Psychotherapist, latterly working at the Portman Clinic, London, where she was particularly interested in children who, unable to access thought, use activity and bodily responses in order to cope with perceived threats. She is a former Head of Training at the British Association of Psychotherapists, has edited the *Journal of Child Psychotherapy*, the official journal of the British Association of Psychotherapists, and has developed the Routledge series on Independent Approaches with Children and Adolescents, co-edited with Monica Lanyado, the third volume of which is in press.

Christopher Reeves is a retired Child Psychotherapist and until recently Director of the Squiggle Foundation. From 1976 to 1991 he was first Consultant and later Principal of the Mulberry Bush School. He has written extensively on Winnicott and issues to do with the theory and practice of child psychotherapy and psychoanalysis. He collaborated with Judith Issroff on the book *Donald Winnicott and John Bowlby: Personal and Professional Perspective* (2005, Karnac).

Richard Rollinson was born and brought up in New York. He came to Britain on a Chancellor's Scholarship from City University,

NY, in 1970 and has remained ever since. He began working in residential child care at the Mulberry Bush School, a specialist care environment for emotionally disturbed and damaged children in Oxfordshire, and fifteen years later became its Director. He was subsequently Chair of the Charterhouse Group of Therapeutic Communities. Currently he is an independent Consultant to residential care communities and organizations, and Director of the Planned Environment Therapy Trust.

Jenny Sprince is an organizational Consultant and a Child and Adolescent Psychotherapist specializing in work with looked after children and their carers. She has worked extensively with children, teachers, and care staff in a variety of residential and educational settings as well as with social work departments and private fostering agencies. She is Clinical Director of Placement Support, a company providing psychodynamic consultation and therapeutic services to looked after children and their carers.

Professor Olive Stevenson C.B.E. began her career as a Child Care Officer in Devonshire, following post-graduate training at the London School of Economics and Political Science (LSE) where Clare Winnicott was her tutor. This was in the early 1950s—the heady days of optimism about the Welfare State and, specifically, about the new services for children in care, made possible by the Children Act 1948. Clare had been a Psychiatric Social Worker in Oxfordshire and had worked with very disturbed children and young people who had been evacuated. Donald Winnicott was a Consultant to the hostels in which such children were placed. The course at the LSE was blazing a trail to improve care for such children. Clare was at its centre but Donald played an important part in it. Although Olive Stevenson's own intellectual and professional development took her over the years to different places and settings, she kept in touch with the Winnicotts throughout the rest of their lives and they continued to influence her profoundly.

Following her period as a Child Care Officer in the 1950s, Olive Stevenson held a number of lecturing and later professorial posts in Bristol, Oxford, Keele, and Nottingham, where she is Professor Emeritus in Social Work. She has been on a number of important Government Commissions, including the Inquiry and Report into the death of Maria Colwell in 1973 and a Commission of Inquiry into Abuse of Elderly and Vulnerable Adults in 1993. Further details of her career and a list of her many publications can be found on her website: www.olivestevenson.com.

Professor Judith Trowell is an Honorary Consultant Psychiatrist, Tavistock Clinic, and Professor of Child Mental Health, West Midlands Institute of Mental Health and Society at the University of Worcester. She is a former Chair of Trustees of YoungMinds and now Chair of Trustees of VOICE. A Psychoanalyst and Child Analyst she worked for many years in the National Health Service as a clinician, trainer, and clinical researcher. Her publications include *The Emotional Needs of Young Children and Their Families: Applications of Psychoanalysis in Community Settings* (with Marion Bower) (1996) and *The Importance of Fathers: A Psychoanalytic Re-Evaluation* (with Alicia Etchegoyen) (2001).

Adrian Ward has a wide-reaching experience of practice and leadership in residential child care, and of training and consultation for this work. Until recently he was a Consultant in Social Work at the Tavistock Clinic, where he was Organizing Tutor for the MA course in Social Work, run jointly with the University of East London. Previously he held similar posts at the University of East Anglia and Reading. He has written and published a number of books and papers, the most recent of which being *Relationship Based Social Work: Getting to the Heart of Practice* (edited with Gillian Ruch and Danielle Turney), 2010, Jessica Kingsley Publishers, London. Further details can be found at: www.adrianward.org.uk.

EDITOR'S INTRODUCTION

Christopher Reeves

"Those who cannot remember the past are condemned to repeat it."

—George Santayana, *The Life of Reason* (1905, p. 284)

The six lectures that make up the bulk of this latest volume in the occasional series of Winnicott Studies Monographs comprise the texts of lectures given in London for the Squiggle Foundation from 2008 to 2010. All but one were specially invited papers on the theme of what Winnicott—disliking some of the connotations of terms such as "deviance" and "delinquency"—chose to call "the antisocial tendency". In preparing them the speakers were given no specific brief in relation to this theme, nor did they have the benefit of knowing what the other speakers would be saying or had said. Inevitably, therefore, some repetition of explanations of concepts and background will be evident over the course of these lectures, as well as some duplication of observations. However, as initiator of the project in my capacity as Director of the Squiggle Foundation at the time, and as editor of the volume, I have resisted the urge to engage the speakers in wholesale revision of their texts as first delivered, either in terms of style or content. Thus the direct conversational tone has been preserved, thereby enabling the reader to get a sense of participation as though a member of the audience when the lectures were being delivered.

As to content, here a different sort of editorial decision was called for. Immediacy and topicality are necessary ingredients of a good lecture, but they are constantly changing. I wrote the first draft of this Introduction in the late summer of 2011 while the attention of the news media in Britain was fastened on the outbreak of rioting, looting, and destruction in the wake of a shooting incident in North London and on the angry and perplexed reactions of the public to these events. Phrases like "a broken society", "the demise of the family", and "loss of social cohesion" fell from the lips of politicians, police, and judiciary. I was well aware that readers of this volume would naturally be inclined to wonder what the opinions of the several contributors might be concerning this troubling episode and its aftermath. Yet when giving their lectures a year or more previously they had no knowledge of what was to take place in August 2011. I decided not to invite them to revisit their texts in the light of these events. My reason was simple. I concluded that what they have to say in these pages is testimony enough to their undoubted concern, not just about the possibility of such an outbreak, but about what was likely to follow when it did, namely, the angrily reactive manner in which judgement would be passed on the perpetrators and the vengeful feelings that would be given free rein by politicians, press, and public alike. They were not making predictions, but they were being sadly prophetic. Wisdom before is more potent in retrospect than wisdom after the event.

Donald Winnicott, Paediatrician, Psychiatrist, and Psychoanalyst, was a shrewd and unsentimental observer of the society of his day, both of its attributes and its ills. He was well aware that antisocial behaviour was antagonistic at its core, and that the feelings of revenge which it provoked had to be acknowledged and met. Yet he was far from accepting the inevitability of family breakdown or social strife. As doctor and advocate of the child in the family, he urged the importance of anticipating breakdown wherever possible, believing that trust, the cement of all relationships, is best secured by foresight and prevention rather than by pity and reparation, and he believed that the same principle obtained in community relations and relations between nations as well. Yet he was also realistic enough to know that human societies and their leaders are not usually prescient in regard to potential catastrophes nor always sensible in dealing with their aftermath, any more than families are. Greed, grandiosity, revenge, or just the imperatives of the moment, can too easily blind the individual, the family, and the group. Almost three-quarters of a century ago Winnicott and Bowlby jointly warned the government of the day about the dangers of precipitately separating children from their families through the proposed evacuation scheme. The scheme went ahead unmodified. Much of their later professional careers was devoted to proposing solutions for some of its foreseeable but unforeseen psychological consequences.

In this series, dedicated to Winnicott's memory forty years after his death, a similar concern animates its authors, both to draw attention to some social and civil dangers implicit in the pursuit of precipitate policy initiatives affecting the family and young people, and to propose remedial action once the consequences have become apparent. However, the contributors have resisted the temptation to say glibly: "We warned you!" These lectures aim to encourage concerted reflection on urgent social issues from a position of shared uncertainty about the best way ahead, not to propose solutions from an imagined higher ground.

While leaving the content of these lectures unchanged, I have nevertheless taken two editorial liberties. I have rearranged the order in which they were originally given and I have included a postscript. We start with Adrian Ward's comprehensive survey of Winnicott's concept of "the antisocial tendency" and its theoretical and practical implications as regards treatment. There follows Professor Olive Stevenson's very personal appraisal of Winnicott as teacher and mentor, and of the continuing relevance (as well as the limitations) of his work on the antisocial tendency. What makes her contribution especially revealing is not only her long personal acquaintance with Donald and Clare Winnicott, but also her wide experience of social work spanning many decades and encompassing all its aspects—practice, teaching, and the formulation of public policy. My own contribution completes the mainly theoretical first half of the volume. In it I first consider the matrix that underpins the structure of Winnicott's thinking about the relationship of child to family, and family to society, and then examine how these interrelationships have evolved both during his life and since his death, with government rather than family becoming increasingly seen as the fulcrum.

I have described these first three lectures as covering the theoretical part, with the remaining three devoted mainly to praxis. Yet Ann Horne's contribution, focusing as it does on the role and limits of individual therapy within a clinic setting for the treatment of antisocial youngsters, also extends the theoretical input in regard to clinical practice. She begins with a detailed review of the psychoanalytic literature, past and present, as it relates to the subject of delinquency, including a consideration of this particular theory's interconnectedness with, and differences from, the more sociological and criminological theories prevalent today. In the course of her examination she challenges one of the central, but controversial, tenets of Winnicott, namely that the antisocial act is (or rather, can be) an expression of hope, while teasing out a productive central element of it, namely that the delinquent act is an expressive act—it is saying something that requires to be heard and responded to appropriately. She also endorses Winnicott's view about the primacy of "therapeutic management" in the treatment of the young delinquent.

The theme of therapeutic management leads naturally onto the last two lectures. Jenny Sprince (whose contribution is introduced by Judith Trowell) considers a vital aspect of such management in a residential setting, namely how within a therapeutic community context responsiveness to the gesture rather than reactivity to challenge can be cultivated, and what support structures have to be put in place for this to happen and for the individual and the community to be reliably sustained. Then Richard Rollinson offers a lively and provocative piece of what he describes as a type of Winnicottian "playing with ideas". In the course of it he turns the standard polarities of debate about antisocial behaviour upside down. He invites us to consider what antisocial, even criminal (although condoned), behaviour of certain *soi-disant* responsible adults—among them bankers, newspaper magnates, business people, and politicians—young people often labelled "antisocial" might be reacting to. He goes on further to ask whether the undoubtedly irresponsible behaviour of many alienated young people, the object of so much current concern, could be due to a failure on the part of the wider society and its guardians to find a means of attuned and appropriate acknowledgement of their disenfranchised situation, as well as for many of them, of their precarious social and economic predicament.

Finally comes Adrian Ward's postscript, one which could not have been written when these lectures were originally given. In it he provides a clinically objective account of the disturbing sequence of events that shook London and other cities in August 2011 and offers some pertinent reflections on them, shaped and given point by some of the ideas and themes expounded in the preceding lectures.

Cornwall,
November 2011

Learning to live with the antisocial tendency: the challenge of residential care and treatment

Adrian Ward

Introduction

This paper explores Donald Winnicott's formulation of "the antisocial tendency" in terms of its implications for the residential care and treatment of children and adolescents. In the context of the political "hot potato" of antisocial behaviour it is instructive to return to Winnicott's conceptualization of the issues in terms of the emotional needs of young people, the origin of these in early childhood, and the ways in which they may be triggered, and by this route to gain clues about helpful ways to respond to young people. The other contextual element is the more recent but incontrovertible evidence about the mental health needs of young people in the care system, many of whom may be viewed as having a "conduct disorder", which as we shall see is very close to the concept of "the antisocial tendency".

Winnicott was unusual in many ways, and especially, for the purposes of this paper, in that he had direct experience through consultancy of the needs of children in residential care. During World War II he became responsible for a group of five hostels for particularly troubled children evacuated from London, and with Clare Britton, whom he was later to marry, he provided support and consultancy to the staff and heads of those hostels. He wrote a number of papers based on this experience and in particular his article on Residential Management as Therapy (Winnicott & Britton, 1947) remains one of the few papers from that era which still speaks directly to today's residential practitioners.

Winnicott's influence on residential care has also been strongly felt through the work of Barbara Dockar-Drysdale at both the Mulberry Bush School and the Cotswold Community. Dockar-Drysdale got to know Winnicott in 1954 and used him as a consultant in the early days of the Mulberry Bush. She brought many of his insights into her practice, most notably in terms of the ideas of "ego-integration" and "unintegration", and concepts of "holding" and "regression". I will return to her work later.

The paper will begin with a brief recapitulation of Winnicott's account of early development in infancy and its implications for subsequent development. Within this context I will outline what he meant by "antisocial tendency" and try to distinguish between, first, this general tendency, second, the persistence of antisocial acts in some young people, and, third, the risk of descent into delinquency. We will examine Winnicott's striking portrayal of "delinquency as a sign of hope" and from there we will consider the implications of this formulation for residential treatment, looking at issues of assessment, everyday living, and the quality of tolerance, and then at the central therapeutic role of individual relationships with young people. Finally we will reflect on the implications of this approach for the self of the worker.

The antisocial tendency: its origins and development

Winnicott on the infant and ego-integration

In simplified terms, Winnicott saw the infant at birth as not yet having a formed ego but of being a "bundle of instincts" and impulses, including "primal fears", such as the fear of going to pieces or falling forever (Winnicott, 1965, p. 58). The baby has a natural tendency towards growing and maturing, and in the vast majority of cases this happens through the loving devotion of the parent, normally the mother, who holds the baby's experience together in a way which ultimately enables the baby to hold him- or her-*self* together through establishing an ego. This is the process which he called "ego-integration", literally the bringing together of bits of experience and awareness, bodily and mental, conscious and unconscious, into a relatively organized and stable whole.

What is most critical in this process is that the mother enables the baby to thrive within this state of absolute dependence, through providing what Winnicott calls a *"good-enough"* environment (1941, p. 67)—meaning that the mother doesn't have to be perfect or get it right every time, but does have to provide an overall good-enough experience which the baby can internalize and use as the basis for a fundamentally healthy orientation towards both self and others. It is this process of ego-integration which is the foundation of the individual's subsequent mental health.

Building on this early experience, the baby very gradually develops out from this relatively short time of total dependence into a more autonomous and rather less dependent existence, as he or she develops the capacity to relate healthily with others in their environment, first within the family and then beyond into the outside world. This second stage in the maturational process is the foundation of the child's growing ability to relate with the social world.

If the very earliest experience does not work well enough and the baby is unable to form a sound relationship with the mother for whatever reason, the capacity to develop a secure ego is undermined and the child may be left prone to those primal fears and anxieties, unable to relate positively and securely with parental figures and thus without a sound basis on which to relate to the social world in which he has to live. Alternatively, the baby may cope with the ever-present chaos and fears by developing a false self, built upon compliance and equally unsound as a basis for relationships.

These are most serious propositions and much of Winnicott's work deals with the consequences of such early distortion or disruption of experience, and with the ways in which therapeutic experience at a later stage may help to repair the damage. His focus on regressive emotional states, for example, deals with the way in which if we have had an early failure of experience we will, when under stress in later life, tend to regress emotionally to the point at which things went wrong, in an unconscious attempt to re-live and hopefully re-work the experience towards a better outcome.

He also makes a critical distinction between what he terms "privation" and "deprivation" (Winnicott, 1956, p. 309). "Privation" refers to the situation just described in which those very earliest needs have not been met, such that the child is just unable to develop an ego and may be prone to psychosis and other related states. "Deprivation", on the other hand, refers to things going wrong at a slightly later stage, when the child has made a secure enough beginning but when some subsequent and serious failure in care or experience leaves the child with a sense of incompleteness, inadequacy, and personal insecurity, and perhaps thereby with a sense of permanent yearning for what they once had, however fleetingly and however unconsciously, but of which they have then been deprived—and perhaps later still they become more troubled (or troubled again) by this deprivation.

The antisocial tendency

Since the theme of this paper is the antisocial tendency one might expect that we will be focusing on those children whose earliest start in life was particularly disastrous and who may be incapable of sustaining themselves in relation to their own mental processes and especially in relation to other people. However, Winnicott was always precise, although sometimes quite idiosyncratic, in his terminology, and he reserved the phrase "the antisocial *tendency*" for a specific scenario.

The first thing to be clear about is that he sees the antisocial tendency as being universal: in a refreshingly "normal" way he acknowledges that every child has, in effect, both social and antisocial tendencies. At this point I must ask those readers whose own childhood was without blemish to "look away now"—those who never deliberately swore, broke anything, shouted at their dear mother, or pushed their sibling off his or her perch from time to time. Winnicott's point is that, as he says:

> A normal child, if he has confidence in father or mother, pulls out all the stops. In the course of time he tries out his power to disrupt, to destroy, to frighten, to wear down, to waste, to wangle and to appropriate. Everything that takes people to the courts (or to the asylums, for that matter) has its normal equivalence in infancy and early childhood, in the relation of the child to his own home. If the home can stand up to all that the child can do to disrupt it, he settles down to play.

> (Winnicott, 1984, p. 115)

Not just to play, of course, but to live a life, although for Winnicott the capacity to play was of enormous importance. And naturally this process of challenge and reconciliation is not a one-off process but a repeated set of tests and challenges through which the child needs to establish what the boundaries of self and autonomy really are—and each time that the boundaries expand a bit as the child grows up, the testing out may have to be repeated. So long as the boundaries are there, offering both a sense of being held but also of the potential for further growth and development, the antisocial tendency remains simply that—the capacity for challenge and perhaps "devilment", for independent thought and even, I would suggest, also for creativity—although Winnicott finds the roots of that more in play.

Winnicott also had much to say about the role of the father in terms of providing clear boundaries and the security within which the original relationship with mother may flourish. Of course, patterns of family and societal expectations have changed enormously since Winnicott's day, and around gender roles in particular, so these stereotyped distinctions between paternal and maternal roles may need re-examining.

However, if the child's challenges don't meet any or enough resistance, if the boundaries are not sufficiently holding but are either absent or, on the other hand, too rigid, then the story is quite different—the child is left unclear, un-held, and without the sense of safe autonomy and personal freedom which should have come from living within a secure relational framework. The instinct and need for boundaries and for the security which they offer remains, however, and the child's search for these emerges in other forms.

In the first place, this search for boundaries may be shown in the family, and in the form of stealing, disrupting, or doing other things which will draw attention to himself, giving him some sense (however negative) of agency in the world. But if the boundaries are not found in the family, these same behaviours may emerge at school or out on the street. As Winnicott (1984, p. 116) says: "The antisocial child is merely looking a little farther afield, looking to society instead of to his own family or school to provide the stability he needs if he is to pass through the early and quite essential stages of his emotional growth."

It is as if, in Jan Abram's words, "the individual is searching for an environment that will say *no*—not in a punitive way, but in a way that will create a sense of security" (Abram, 2007, p. 54; my emphasis). This is largely an unconscious search of course, in which the child is repeatedly driven to seek out something which is instinctively felt to be missing.

Delinquency as a sign of hope

Here we come to the central element in Winnicott's thesis, which is summed up in his phrase "delinquency as a sign of hope" (Winnicott, 1967). The argument is that the antisocial tendency is found in children who *have* had a good enough start but for whom things have not developed so well from there on—so they are left with the tantalizing sense that things could be better but that they don't consciously know *what* could be better or how to achieve that. This is why the initial appearance of delinquency in the form of the antisocial tendency is seen as a sign of hope—because there is an implication in the child's actions that they instinctively know that things are not right for them, that things could be different and better—and that indeed they once *were* different and better.

These antisocial acts can now be read as an unconscious expression of the need to go back to that lost state of security and of feeling held. Such a child's greatest need is to encounter the metaphorical enclosing arms of a loving boundary—one which will certainly say no, but which will do that without taking retribution or causing further damage; one which will hear the communication behind the delinquent act, and offer a response which reaches the need hidden within it.

This was and still remains one of Winnicott's most remarkable and profound insights, and one which has had considerable impact, for better or worse. We all know about the public thirst for retribution in relation to delinquency and how important it is to be able to articulate a very different position.

So when trying to make sense of antisocial behaviour we always need to ask ourselves what a given delinquent act signifies—Why *that* act rather than another? Why *now*? Why *this* young person, in that situation, at that time? What may they have been hoping for? There is a whole spectrum of the antisocial tendency (which is why the term "tendency" is so rich and so apt).

It will sometimes be the case that there is some particular symbolism in the antisocial act—and, for instance, Winnicott makes a clear distinction between stealing as a form of seeking love, and destruction as a way of testing the environment's capacity to tolerate. But there may be more significance in terms of the quality of longing or a deeply hidden sense of loss and deprivation which the act indicates—and which it may equally evoke in others. What is critical for the young person is that the act needs to convey something to someone in a form which will be heard. If it is unheard it simply remains an act; if it is heard it realizes its potential as a communication.

Many minor antisocial acts will be heard and contained within the family, and many others within the school or other institutions, but if this does not achieve what the child needs, the antisocial tendency spreads out into society as a whole, with stealing, petty vandalism, drug-taking, drunkenness, and everything else which follows. And unfortunately, the further it spreads beyond those who do know and have any relationship with the child, the less likely it is that the act will be heard as a communication and the more likely that it will evoke a harsh punitive response from society and its representatives.

This is where the antisocial tendency begins to turn into real delinquency: if the hoped-for communication does not develop, because the act is read as solely negative rather than partly positive, things become more serious, and reactions harden on both sides.

> By the time the boy or girl has become hardened because of the failure of communication, the antisocial act not being recognised as something that contains an SOS [MAYDAY], and when secondary gains have become important, and great skill has been achieved in some antisocial activity, then it is much more difficult to see (what is still there, nevertheless) the SOS that is a signal of hope in the boy or girl who is antisocial.
>
> (Winnicott, 1967, p. 90)

So we have moved from something hopeful to something much less hopeful, although it is essential to recognize the point added in parenthesis here—that the hope is still there. It is that hidden hope and the confused and confusing signals which it sends out that we will need to seek out when trying to help these young people.

Young people in residential care

At this point we need to move from the general to the particular and from this widening societal scenario to the painful situations in which many young people in the care system find themselves.

If we think of the life stories of most of the young people being looked after in fostering or residential care, there is every likelihood that they will have experienced the kinds of deprivation which we have been considering. Of course some of them will have experienced the more serious *privation* such that they have little capacity to hold themselves together at all, but I would suggest that many of them will come within the broad category of the antisocial tendency and its more serious stage of delinquency.

The evidence for this statement can be found in the always-shocking figures on the mental health needs of young people in the looked after system. The proportion of children in residential care with mental health difficulties of all kinds go as high as 70% and above (Meltzer, Corbin, Gatward, Goodman & Ford, 2002), and a good proportion of these come under the heading of "conduct disorder", a diagnostic category whose symptoms could easily have appeared under Winnicott's list of antisocial acts: lying, stealing, delinquent acts of violence and destruction, etc. In many cases these mental health needs have never been properly assessed and diagnosed and no form of psychiatric or psychotherapeutic help has been offered. This powerful data is at last finding its way through into policy in various forms.

In the rest of this paper I will examine the implications of Winnicott's writings on the antisocial tendency for some aspects of working with young people in residential care. This is a large and complicated subject so I will focus on a few basic points, beginning with assessment, moving onto an aspect of daily living, and then to the theme of tolerance. I will focus especially on the core relationship between the young person and his or her residential carer, and finally on the further implications of this model for the self of the individual worker. What I have to say builds upon the best practice in therapeutic care settings, although, given the very high figures just mentioned, it is clear to me that all residential care should include some element of therapeutic work.

Assessment

The first point is that children and young people in residential care need to be assessed. Without an agreed and well-founded way of assessing their emotional needs we cannot make proper provision to meet those needs. There is an approach to the assessment of children's emotional needs based upon Winnicott's work which Barbara Dockar-Drysdale formulated at the Mulberry Bush School many years ago and which was in use at the Cotswold Community for a long time, although it is not currently in use in either place. One version of this assessment focused on the needs of unintegrated children and one on integrated children (Dockar-Drysdale, 1993). For our purposes today we might think more about the Needs Assessment for Integrated Children. There will not be space here to go into the details, but the critical point is that this is an approach to assessment which consists of working at understanding the child's needs rather than merely cataloguing their behaviours.

Another valuable aspect of the Needs Assessment is that it is worked upon collectively in a staff meeting of the child's immediate residential carers, drawing extensively on their own lived experience with the young person. The value of this process is that it also therefore provides a staff development function, as it enables the staff team to work together on pooling their own experiences of each child and making sense of them in relation to theoretical concepts, leading to new understandings which can then feed directly back into their daily work.

Such an assessment will hopefully enable the team to concentrate very closely on the young person's inner world—their deep personal experience of their lives both in terms of their history and their current anxieties. This concentration helps to build a sense of attunement with the young person through which the staff team collectively may be able to work together to provide an emotional climate or environment in which the young person may be able to feel less anxious, less defensive, more in touch with their own feelings, and more able to relate with people on a more real level.

The theory is that, through this very careful provision of the sort of emotional experiences which the child has missed out on in earlier life, the child can be helped to feel safe enough to return to the point of failure, and back beyond that to the sort of feelings which were once the basis of their security. If they can re-experience those feelings in a new and safer way they may then be able to hold on to a great feeling of security and not need to be driven by their unconscious yearning for Paradise Lost, or to enact all sorts of antisocial feelings in order to draw attention to themselves.

Managing everyday life

Young people in this situation may appear highly volatile and unpredictable, subject to what are often called "rapid mood swings". This can make life in residential care settings fairly difficult at times, but for the moment I want to focus on the individual need behind the behaviour rather than on other aspects of managing the everyday life of the group in residential care.

In fact, the more closely we concentrate on understanding the *individual* young person's emotional needs the less unpredictable their behaviour is likely to become—even though the young person him- or herself may still experience their own feelings as unpredictable. We may discover that there are certain kinds of feeling which predominate for the young person or which are triggered by particular kinds of interaction with other people, whether peers or family members. This might be as simple as flaring up when some particular request is made of them, such as getting up in the morning, or when being challenged by a peer, or when being reminded of some aspect of their family relationships.

Barbara Dockar-Drysdale showed that if we get to know the young person really well, we may be able to help them discover and understand their particular patterns and triggers, their own proneness to certain types of reaction. This will probably require us to concentrate very hard on our assessments and to share our perceptions with colleagues to make sense of them, and this is why the assessment always needs to focus on understanding the needs rather than merely describing the behaviour.

If we can help the young person in this way—helping them to understand and predict their own behaviour more accurately—it can make an enormous difference to their daily lives, because they may begin to feel more in charge of themselves and less at the mercy of their own storms and tempests. This is a way of helping them to rebuild and repair ego-function: organizing experience, regulating their own emotions, and learning to consciously anticipate difficulties and powerful feelings. This process of learning to anticipate is painstaking but it is a direct way in which we can contribute to their mental health.

Tolerance

I was reminded recently when reading a paper by Damien McLellan (2010) of the radical proposition of doing child care without punishment. This is a very challenging proposition, because we are all prone to vengeful angry feelings, especially if it is *our* car that has been scratched, our face that has been punched by a delinquent young person, or our patience that has been worn to breaking point. The mood of vengeance in public discourse is extremely powerful and seems to have become more so in recent years, often fed on behalf of society by the press and politicians. But we have to be very careful when working with emotionally vulnerable young people not to confuse boundaries with punishment, and especially not to confuse it with vengeance.

We may believe that young people have *"got to learn"*, as a former colleague of mine used to repeat many times a day, but maybe it is also *we* who have to learn how to do child care differently, how to enable the young people to realize things for themselves, how to discover or rediscover their own sense of right and wrong. This may come about through a range of means such as direct communication about feelings and the requirement on them to think through the morals of their behaviour.

It may also come about, however, through what for most of them will be the surprising experience of being still regarded warmly and even affectionately despite their horribly challenging behaviours. Our aim will be to find a way of getting past their familiar experiences of anger and acting-out, and helping them to learn to reflect on the underlying anxieties which may have been driving their experience.

A certain degree of tolerance also has the effect of enabling symptoms of anxiety or concern to emerge and be communicated which might otherwise remain hidden and unexpressed. This may be especially difficult in the current climate of regulation and inspection where every last detail of behaviour and risk is supposed to be reported and "actioned", but unless we can show some genuine tolerance (and if necessary take some genuine risks) we will not get far in helping the most troubled children.

Individual relationship

At the heart of any therapeutic work with a young person will be the relationship, the core relationship, which in classical psychotherapy will be with the psychotherapist but in residential care is likely to be with one of the residential carers, perhaps supervised by a therapist.

We need to remember that what will make a difference to the young person in the long run will be that within an environment of well-boundaried loving care there was someone in particular who understood them—this is what we all remember from school, hospitals, and most other experiences of groups and institutions—whether there was a benign regime and a supportive peer group and whether there was somebody who really cared about us. In residential work it is likely to be with one of the residential carers that the child wishes to form a special bond.

There is much anxiety these days around the nature of therapeutic relationships for young people because of the scandals of exploitation and abuse in the recent past, although we can largely address those anxieties through good supervision and management and an open culture. There is also a certain amount of avoidance in some residential settings of special relationships because of anxieties about what can realistically be provided by staff without formal therapeutic training—will they get themselves into deep water? The fact is that within the context of a well-managed and supervised team, individual staff can and do offer young people profoundly important relationships. This has certainly been the experience of myself and many others in relation to therapeutic child care settings.

Bearing in mind what we have just covered in relation to the antisocial tendency, what the young person is likely to need is someone who will reliably hear the communication behind their antisocial acts. The advantage for the residential worker is that because they are in the thick of it with the young person they may be a witness of, or even a victim of, the antisocial act, which means that they are in a position to feel aggrieved but to not take revenge, or to be appalled but to not exact punishment. This is in some ways the ideal position because they are clearly in both a parenting and a therapeutic role: not so *un*involved as to be of little significance to the young person, but at the same time not actually the young person's parent. If they know and understand the young person well enough they are very well placed to offer exactly what is required: a response based upon hearing the communication behind the act.

Responding to the antisocial act

There is considerable skill, of course, in offering such a response, and I am not just thinking in terms of straight interpretation—we all know about Winnicott's (1971, p. 68) cautious remarks about "clever interpretation": "[T]he significant moment is that at which the child surprises him or herself. It is not the moment of my clever interpretation."

What may be needed is a response which is oriented towards inviting communication rather than towards the more obvious reactions to "bad behaviour", such as: "How dare you?" or "What do you think you're doing?" or "Why did you do that?" Challenges like those are highly likely to bring stereotyped retorts or further escalation.

Somehow we need to get right behind the acts to focus on the communication, or on the need for communication, or the yearning to feel that one has once again the capacity for communication and has access to someone with whom that communication may be possible.

This may mean finding other ways to convey to the young person a willingness to listen, such as sitting quietly with them after some explosion or distress and perhaps offering them some bodily comfort such as a hot drink or a blanket. There may have been some "delinquent merger" in which two or more young people have become lost in the excitement of one another's delinquency and they may need to be offered quite different and separate things to help them re-establish their own non-delinquent identity.

The question of basic physical needs is of great importance. Very often in the situation of an individual or group antisocial act which has turned into panicky delinquency I found myself remembering Dockar-Drysdale's phrase about "converting delinquent excitement into oral greed" (Dockar-Drysdale, 1961, p. 170; see also Hancock, Simmons & Whitwell, 1990), and steering young people towards the kitchen where it may be possible to offer them sustenance, which would often have the effect not of refuelling them for further delinquency but of putting them back in touch with their own body and their innermost feelings—quite often their sadness and longing.

What lies beyond the establishment of communication is a whole other story, and on some occasions the communication may lead to the young person disclosing a wide range of other anxieties—or sometimes it may lead nowhere except that the young person may have had the unusual and special experience—for them—of being able to recognize and express their feelings rather than acting them out. This is how relationships of trust are built and how the regenerative process of therapeutic support for young people is developed.

For the residential worker the challenge is that they do have to manage everyday life, promote social harmony, and a facilitating environment, while also tolerating a certain amount of acting-out if that is the only way that feelings will get expressed, but also hold in place the boundaries—while nevertheless listening out for the deeper communications which may lie behind some of the behaviour. It's rocket science—not least because if the mixture is wrong or the trajectory out of line, it may be truly explosive!

Using the relationship

While the care relationship in residential care is primarily that—one of caring—it may be possible for the young person to use the relationship with their primary residential carer in an equivalent way to the way in which some young people use their psychotherapist.

In some places this will be "managed" through a series of individual sessions or what may be called "special times" when the child is guaranteed time and space with that carer, away from the demands of everyday life, to think and talk or play or paint or whatever feels right, and in some places this will be supervised as formal therapeutic practice.

In other places it will happen in the course of everyday life, especially through what I call "opportunity-led work"—where the opportunities for meaningful communication may arise out of everyday experiences and incidents. The skill for the worker lies in spotting and using these opportunities in a way which will feel real and supportive for the young person. We saw earlier that sometimes young people's strong feelings will be revived or triggered by apparently trivial everyday events, and that there may be a barely discernible pattern to these reactions or sequences of feelings. Like gazing at a night sky, the unfamiliar observer will detect little or nothing by way of patterns, whereas the experienced eye will find many connections and patterns.

The carer may sometimes be able to help the young person recognize such patterns within themselves, and this sort of support may be particularly helpful if it can be offered in the heat of the moment or just after an incident or communication, which of course is where the residential context offers many opportunities.

In particular, it may be that what the carer can spot is what Winnicott calls the "hopeful moment" (1956, p. 314): that coming together in the young person of the drive towards seeking communication and sensing the potential within the relational environment for this to be expressed and hopefully to find a response. That is the aim of the residential worker in caring for young people with the antisocial tendency.

Use of self

What we have to be prepared for if we are going to work in this way is that we will also encounter our own most powerful anxieties and defences, and our own antisocial tendencies. This is inevitable if we are working with such strong feelings in others. Strong feelings are infectious. Rather like being with someone who keeps yawning, although of course at a much more serious level, we are likely to find our own equilibrium unsettled (and not always in obvious or conscious ways) by the close and persistent contact with the young people's trauma— and in this case not because it is so different from our own feelings, but because it is so *similar* to some of our own feelings, even though we may have learned to deal with these in different ways.

Even in writing this paper I struggled for quite a long time as I tried to avoid getting put back in touch with the struggles in my own childhood and adolescence which led me to spend my adult life thinking about these very themes. If it's true, as I'm sure it is, that we all know about the antisocial tendency from within, from our own internal experience, then it may also be true that if we have chosen to work in this whole arena of helping other people in distress, and have stayed in it, we have probably found a way to make creative and productive use of our antisocial tendency, to convert it into something quite different— something creative rather than destructive, something which involves giving rather than stealing. It may be a round-about way to carry on seeking for our own lost Golden Age, but it is generally a lot healthier than the alternative.

The fact that we may have had these difficulties and struggles in our own past doesn't disqualify us at all from working in this field, so long as we have had—and continue to have—the opportunity to reflect upon and rework our own experience. In fact this is an aspect of our selves which we should value and nurture, because it is often the basis on which we are able and willing to offer young people the sort of empathic and tolerant help which I have described here: if we can tolerate our own trauma and distress we will be much better placed to tolerate that of others. As Robin Skynner (1989, pp. 160–173) said in this context: "Don't kill the goose that lays the golden eggs."

For this reason I feel it is essential that if we are going to work with people who are seriously antisocial, we should have proper supervision, which covers not only the discussion of "the case" and the procedural aspects of the work, but also the emotional experience of doing this work. This supervision must help us to recognize and realize what it means to us to get so close to such painful feelings. For example, I have spoken about the need to respond rather than to retaliate and to tolerate rather than to punish—none of this is lightly done. We need to be very clear about these sorts of boundaries, and about how we deal with our own more punitive instincts, or our outrage, at having been insulted or spat upon. It is not always a good idea to spit back, of course, although I know of more than one worker who has found themselves doing just that. If we end up having to swallow our pride and our anger, let alone our own spittle, we need to pay attention to what that may be doing to us.

On the other hand, I am by no means arguing for the sort of leniency which suggests a lack of boundaries and which will be experienced by many delinquent youngsters as utterly provocative. We certainly need to be able to say no and to use real authority in doing so, and we may also need to find ways of letting the young person know about some of our feelings and thus letting them know how we have managed them. So to say "When you spat in my face this evening I felt like throttling you" may be dramatic, but it may be a lot more real and healthy than either saying nothing or just letting rip with anger.

Finally, we always need to keep in mind that in the residential setting there is always *the group* of young people and *the team* of staff to keep in mind, and the group-based interactions and the flow of conscious and unconscious feeling between these groups. Although much of Winnicott's focus is on the one-to-one communications between the young person and other individuals, in residential care there is always a group dynamic at play, too, and indeed much of the anti*social* may be expressed as anti*group*. This is a whole other field of study which we will not have time to consider in this paper.

Conclusion

There is much more that could and perhaps should have been said—and in particular I have said nothing about working with the families of the young people and the critical task of helping the young people where possible to re-establish some sort of relationship with their family. What I have tried to concentrate on is the way in which the particular dynamic of the antisocial tendency finds its way into the residential setting, but also on the opportunities which this setting uniquely offers to respond creatively to young people's unconscious search for communication. This is the challenge represented in the title.

References

Abram, J. (2007). *The Language of Winnicott: A Dictionary of Winnicott's Use of Words* (2nd edn). London: Karnac.

Dockar-Drysdale, B. (1961). The problem of making adaptations to the needs of the individual child in a group. In: *The Provision of Primary Experience* (pp. 167–177). London: Free Association Books.

Dockar-Drysdale, B. (1993). *Therapy and Consultation in Child Care*. London: Free Association Books.

Hancock, P., Simmons, S. & Whitwell, J. (1990). The importance of food in relation to the treatment of deprived and disturbed children in care. *International Journal of Therapeutic Communities, 11(2)*: 103–111.

McLellan, D. (2010). Why a therapeutic community approach to residential child care? *International Journal of Child & Family Welfare, 13(3/4)*: 116–122.

Meltzer, H., Corbin, T., Gatward, R., Goodman, R. & Ford, T. (2002). *The Mental Health of Young People Looked After by Local Authorities in England. Summary Report. A Survey Carried Out by the Social Survey Division of ONS on Behalf of the Department of Health*. London: HMSO.

Skynner, A. C. R. (1989). Make sure to feed the goose that lays the golden eggs: A discussion on the myth of altruism. In: *Institutes and How to Survive Them: Mental Health Training and Consultation* (pp. 160–173). London: Routledge, 1991.

Ward, A. (2008). Opportunity led work. In: B. Luckock & M. Lefevre (Eds.), *Direct Work: Social Work with Children and Young People in Care* (pp. 181–194). London: BAAF.

Winnicott, D. W. (1941). The observation of infants in a set situation. In: *Through Paediatrics to Psychoanalysis* (pp. 52–69). London: Hogarth Press.

Winnicott, D. W. (1956). The antisocial tendency. In: *Through Paediatrics to Psychoanalysis* (pp. 306–315). London: Hogarth Press, 1958.

Winnicott, D. W. (1965). *The Maturational Processes and the Facilitating Environment*. London: Hogarth Press.

Winnicott, D. W. (1967). Delinquency as a sign of hope. In: C. Winnicott, R. Shepherd & M. Davis (Eds.), *Home is Where We Start From* (pp. 90–100). London: Penguin Books, 1986.

Winnicott, D. W. (1971). *Playing & Reality*. London: Tavistock.

Winnicott, D. W. (1984). Some psychological aspects of juvenile delinquency. In: C. Winnicott, R. Shepherd & M. Davis (Eds.), *Deprivation and Delinquency* (pp. 113–119). London: Tavistock.

Winnicott, D. W. & Britton, C. (1947). Residential management as treatment for difficult children. In: C. Winnicott, R. Shepherd & M. Davis (Eds.), *Deprivation and Delinquency* (pp. 54–72). London: Tavistock.

Responses to antisocial youth: does Donald Winnicott have messages for us today?

Olive Stevenson

Introduction: my experience of Donald Winnicott
as friend and mentor

The first part of this paper discusses my understanding of Donald Winnicott's writing about the "antisocial tendency" and, related but distinct, about delinquency. I come to all this from a particular angle and I cannot claim the expertise which many here today will have; I am not a Psychoanalyst nor have I specialized in matters such as forensic psychology or criminology. In fact, even within my professional expertise, that of social work, I have given less time to the issues surrounding "antisocial youth" than some other pressing problems of our time. There are a number of complex reasons for this but one is a deep uncertainty about, and, latterly, repugnance at, the use of this term and at our social responses to this group of young people. The invitation to give a lecture on this theme helped me to face up to my profound concern about the present position in the UK.

The second personal element which affects the content of this paper is, of course, my relationship with Donald and Clare Winnicott. In 1952, Clare was my tutor at the LSE when I took the then pioneering child care course. Both were remarkable teachers. Their home was the centre

19

of splendid parties offering something fresh, exciting, and fun in our grey post-war world. They used these events to mix students with recently qualified social workers, which enhanced a sense of camaraderie in the small group. These two people were the most influential teachers in my life, far outstripping even some excellent tutoring for my first degree in English literature. Looking back (and confirmed by what I have subsequently read about them), I see that they were both essentially creative, artistic people. In some ways they offered a familiar, congenial path to my further intellectual development. Sometimes, Donald was not an "easy read"; many of his theoretical assumptions were then totally unfamiliar to me. But, whether "face-to-face", or, later, in the written word, there were always what I can only call "moments of truth", when impact is immediate, and memorable, in a way which shapes one's further thinking. In this sense, of "the imaginative leap", Donald's writing is at times poetic.

At the time of my LSE studies, the work of, and training for, the Probation Service was separate from the Children's Departments in local authorities, then emerging under the new Children Act 1948. The Probation Service at that time did much more work with children and young people. Structural linkage between services was not made, except in Scotland, but the development of generic training brought the two much closer together in approach. It was, however, symptomatic of the ambivalence, which continued long after generic training included probation, that one often heard that generic courses were "for social workers *and* probation officers". It infuriated me and I thought it would only be a matter of time before the distinction became irrelevant. I was quite wrong. Social work and probation were never married and the engagement was broken off in the 1990s. I read with weary amusement a recent article in the *Guardian* which suggested that probation work had much social work in it.

Back to Donald. He had a great interest in the matters briefly subsumed under the phrase "antisocial tendencies". This was not a particular theme in our teaching at the LSE, which was focused mainly on children in care. But the work which Clare and Donald had done during the war with the seriously disturbed children who had been evacuated to Oxfordshire, included a fair number of delinquent children (as well as those who were psychotic) and pervaded much of their thinking. It recurred again and again, especially in the context of the residential care/management of such children.

Brett Kahr (2006) reminds us that Donald was psychiatrically responsible for 285 evacuated children in Oxfordshire, a good many of whom manifested seriously "antisocial" behaviour.

Donald and Clare, at the time I was a student, were also making links with the emerging work of John Bowlby (1951) on the concept of attachment. For us as students, the film made by James Robertson (1953) on young children separated from their mothers was profoundly significant.

Thus, two ideas, interacting, shaped our thinking: the importance of relationships in early years *and* its connection with subsequent behavioural disturbance. What I did not absorb from Donald at that time were his ideas about the connections between the individual and social forces/trends outside of the family. These, I think, are often found in allusions rather than as fully worked out themes. Sociology and criminology were still closed books to me. I shall return to this later.

Winnicott and the critique of contemporary social policy

The themes from his writing which I have selected to comment on raise critical questions for contemporary social policy. First is the seminal paper written in 1956, "The Antisocial Tendency" (hereafter abbreviated to A.S.T). He makes at the outset a distinction between the terms "A.S.T" and "delinquency". He sees the latter, "delinquency", as an *organized* antisocial *defence* "overloaded with secondary gain and social reactions which make it difficult ... to get to its core". By contrast, "the A.S.T can be studied as it appears in the normal or near normal child, related to the difficulties that are inherent in emotional development" (Winnicott, 1956, p. 306). (I have not been able to keep the two separate in this paper.)

In that one paragraph, we have a crucial but complex theme for policy development. Manifestations of the A.S.T are indications, although not definitive prognoses, of "trouble ahead". They need to be heeded and attended to. If not, they move into delinquency, and harden into patterns which bring gratifications, dangerous to the individual and to society. This assumption lies behind many initiatives in recent years, notably that of Sure Start.

Donald makes two key points about A.S.T. First, he says that "it is characterised by an element in it which compels the environment to be important" (p. 309). He sees the antisocial person's behaviour as unconsciously intended to *force* someone to attend to management; that is, it is a provocation, not simply behaviour which leaves out of account other people's feelings/needs. The second key point about A.S.T. is that it implies hope.

The idea of "hope" as critical is developed in the following: "It (hope) is vital in the treatment of children who show the anti-social tendency. Over and over again, one sees the moment of hope wasted or withered because of mismanagement or intolerance. ... Treatment ... is management, a going to meet and match the moment of hope" (p. 309).

The assertion that antisocial behaviours may be seen as hopeful is related to the idea of *deprivation*, to be distinguished from *privation*. That is, something, which has been good, has been lost; privation means it has never been. Deprivation means that "things went well enough and then they did not go well enough". In such children stealing or destructiveness are two of the "trends" (he does not say "symptoms") one would expect to find. He stresses that their "nuisance value" may be "a favourable feature" because it is a demand for attention. "It is exploited by the child and is not a chance affair" (p. 311).

Donald, therefore, links the manifestation of antisocial behaviours to deprivation. We need first to clear the ground regarding the word "deprivation". The term over the subsequent years has had different and confused connotations. It has been used often to describe children and families in material and environmental poverty, although the word "disadvantage" is now often substituted. Certainly, it has associations that go well beyond the issues of parental attachment which Bowlby developed. The context in which the Winnicotts used it, closely related to Bowlby's work, was mostly about separation of mother/caretaker and child, with resultant loss. This was bound up with wartime and evacuation experiences. However, this led to a consideration of more subtle forms of breakdown and loss in the individual relationships between parent and child, even when the home is not "broken" in the obvious sense. The idea of "emotional deprivation" certainly does not carry with it physical separation as an inevitable component.

Much of the evidence and subsequent debate about the effects of privation and/or deprivation was based on studies of grossly inadequate orphanages or residential nurseries. For *some* of the children there, the emptiness of emotional experience had been so total that it seemed there could not be the "hope" that leads to "antisocial acts". (Donald would have seen such children as unintegrated/psychotic.)

Michael Rutter and colleagues have carried out important longitudinal studies on the impact and outcomes for children from Romanian orphanages who were adopted. The latest (Rutter et al., 2009) raises forty-five questions for policy and practice arising from the research.

Most recently, in my own reflections (Stevenson, 2007) on children seriously neglected in their own homes, especially where there is gross substance abuse by parents, I have been wondering whether *some* of these children may also be in fact "prived" rather than "deprived". That is to say, the parent simply does not have emotional space or time to empathize with the child and to have essential interactions. If such is the case, then the "bad" behaviour which the child exhibits is not, in Winnicottian terms, antisocial behaviour indicating hope. Rather it is part of a battle for survival starting in infancy. This, of course, has very serious implications for policy and practice; just as we have come to understand the crucial importance of removing young children from orphanages to families before irreparable damage is done, so we may have to review our care plans in respect of a significant number of seriously neglected children in their own homes. There are, in fact, some signs of such a shift in thinking.

In any case, returning to the issue of emotional *de*privation, the evidence is now overwhelming that it can adversely affect all aspects of a young child's development, bodily, cognitively, and socially. Donald would have had no difficulty in integrating modern evidence into his theoretical position. But perhaps one can demonstrate more clearly now that such deprivation may impair the very capacities which are usually employed by the child in order to develop into a healthy adult. Thus, the *emotional* stimuli of early mother–child interaction sparks *cognitive* development; the parents who "contain" and "manage" a young child's behaviour begin a child's socialization into what one might call "the rules of the game". This is a crucial point in seeking to understand the link between attachment and the wild, uncontrolled behaviour of certain children from seriously neglectful families.

This leads me back to the difference between Donald's interpretation of the meaning of *"antisocial tendency"* as an attempt to regain what has been lost and the way the phrase is often used today to describe a failure to conform to the norms and values of a given society. Both carry a sense of protest, but whereas it is implicit in Donald's analysis and case illustrations that this protest is directed at the adults within the family, the latter protest seems to be directed at the wider society, which the children and young people feel has failed them. How often do we hear young people "loitering in groups" complain when interviewed on television that "there isn't enough to do round here".

I am not expert enough to do what is required—to make a bridge between the essence of Donald's psychoanalytic understanding and the analysis of the sociologists and criminologists who now dominate the literature on this topic in the UK. To aid my fast-waning confidence about this lecture, I bought a very large book (second-hand), *The Oxford Handbook of Criminology* (4th edn), which has 1139 pages and thirty-two chapters. (It may have been a mistake; it is very heavy.) I was struck by how little, in an excellent and scholarly book, there was space devoted to what we might call "the psychological" (let alone "the psychoanalytical") view of this subject. There is one chapter (Chapter Two) on criminological psychology, where the sections run as follows:

- Early accord
- Psychology and Criminology: The parting of the ways
- Little common ground
- Not on speaking terms
- Return to cordiality?

(Hollin, 2007, pp. 43–47)

In conclusion, the author, Hollin, suggests that psychology of particular kinds (no reference to psychoanalytic) has a significant contribution to make to criminological theory. But that's as far as it goes. It is noticeable that of the thirty-two chapters, only three or four can be said to attend to intra-familial factors in criminal behaviour. This theoretical gulf is a serious barrier to our understanding of juveniles, especially as they enter adolescence.

Bridging the divide: "social ecology"

The dictionary tells me that "schism" implies "factions". While psychoanalysis itself is well used to schisms, the gap between it and sociological perspectives in relation to antisocial behaviour and crime suggests that, rather than a schism, there is a serious lack of *engagement* between psychoanalysis and sociology in this area. This is a huge pity.

I find the notion of "social ecology" some help in bridging the divide, as I have in my work on neglected children (Stevenson, 2007).

I have suggested that we may be more receptive to ideas of social ecology because of our growing awareness of ecological factors, these subtle and extensive interactions, in the worlds of biology and zoology. When we apply these ideas to society and to what we know about the progress of a child from the womb to adulthood, it becomes easier to track the interactions over the years between the family and wider societal factors. The balance of dependence shifts between the two but no-one at a Squiggle Foundation meeting like this would underestimate the continuing effects of earlier familial experiences and deficits. The trick is to avoid psychic determinism. The very fact that there *is* a wider environment *may* offer hope for remedial experiences—as Donald well knew.

But there is also a powerful sociological analysis of the contemporary "woes of youth", in relation to the most worrying aspects of contemporary youth culture.

Such a picture of British youth today is powerfully drawn by John Pitts' (2008) book *Reluctant Gangsters: The Changing Face of Youth Crime*. Using research in British cities, Pitts constructs a typology of gangs. He is emphatic that there are grounds for great concern about this in the UK. It is not, in his view, a case of simply importing anxiety from the US. He is dismissive of what he describes as "crime-averse criminologies". He describes with stinging detail the "concentration of disadvantage" in which certain urban young people live and their affiliation with specific gangs. Young people may be "reluctant affiliates" (Pitts, 2008, p. 101) but membership also serves a number of powerful needs. Affiliation to a gang serves certain purposes:

- affiliation because of the risks to oneself and one's family;
- affiliation because of the risk from other gangs;
- affiliation to gain access to educational/recreational resources in gang territory;
- affiliation because of lack of access to legitimate opportunity;
- continued affiliation because of danger inherent in leaving the gang; and
- psychological dependence.

Pitts argues, in my view convincingly, that most of the different theoretical analyses of "gang affiliation" "fail to recognise the power of the machinery of intimidation and coercion at work in gang-affected neighbourhoods and the choices it necessitates for the young people confined there" (p. 106).

Pitt attacks what he describes as the "individualising imperative" in criminal youth justice (p. 35). Having listed a formidable array of major risk factors associated with gang involvement, all the way from the individual to the community, he concludes: "[I]n practice, it is usually only the individual and familial risk factors to which criminal justice agencies have the capacity to respond and so they come to occupy the foreground" (p. 34) neglecting the wider social factors. So he suggests that the theoretical framework used by those who seek to help neglects the "world outside" and the damage it is doing to the young person. Yet those of us who look at such practice find little to confirm this preoccupation.

It is suggested by those outside that those inside who seek to intervene are blinkered in their understanding, yet those of us also "on the inside" all too frequently criticize the lack of skills in establishing therapeutic relationships based on theories of family and interactions and dynamics. Talk about "can't win"!

Pitts' book says very little about the family background or individual psychology of the young people involved. We are still left with the questions: Which one becomes a reluctant affiliate? What factors play a part in joining the gang?

Pitts is an angry man and in his concluding paragraph he movingly argues that we have separated ourselves from this small but significant part of our youth culture; we look on—they are not us … "We must decide whether they are 'our' young people or not. And if we recognise that they are, we must turn the question of the social, economic and cultural conditions that propel them towards involvement in violent youth gangs into a burning issue" (p. 162).

There, in a nutshell, is my dilemma: how to frame policy and intervention to reflect the range of factors which turn hope into despair, desperation, and full-blown criminality. I am sure that if Donald had read Pitts' book, he would not have been dismissive of what is, essentially, a sociological perspective. He was much too wise for that and his writing contains fascinating references to the world outside of the family and its effects on young people.

The social and economic dimensions of deprivation

But there is a dimension of antisocial behaviour often discussed in relation to social class which raises key questions about equality and inequality of opportunity within our society on which (I think) Donald has little to say. In the period in which he wrote most, when I was beginning my career as a social work teacher, the split between psychoanalytic and sociological theory in the UK was clear. At the LSE (1952–1954), I learnt little or nothing of sociology even within the framework of basic social science. (An attempt to teach me economics failed dismally; I remember being underwhelmed by the overarching presumption that "Rational Man" controlled the economy.) In the early 1960s, I found myself at Oxford surrounded by eminent and able sociologists. My attempt to get my boss A. H. Halsey to give me some sociology tutorials was rejected.

An illustration of one of the lasting effects of this division may be found in the gulf which appeared between Child Guidance Clinics (as they were then called) and local authority children's services. A not-talked-about distinction was evident in the direction of referrals. "Posher" children, whose parents were (say) emotionally neglectful but whose material care was satisfactory, headed for the (then) Child Guidance Clinics, whilst the "grubby" children in generally neglectful conditions might find themselves the "cases" of social services.

Yet it is obvious that both Clare and Donald through their evacuation work were well acquainted with a range of children from all social backgrounds; they were also of the generation who saw a raft of "welfare" legislation designed to reduce inequality, and there is no suggestion of a social pecking order for intervention in Donald's writing. But they were, of course, children of their times and the clientele of psychoanalysts were overwhelmingly middle class.

When I first read "Adolescence: struggling through the doldrums" (1965), it made a lasting impression, which began with that wonderful title! This paper is awash with memorable moments (too many to cite here) including, by the way: "A good motto for any investigator of the subject of sex would be this: whoever asks questions must expect to be told lies" (p. 81). He shows, in references to venereal disease; contraception, and the atomic bomb, to name but three subjects, an intense awareness of the impact on the adolescent of external trends and forces. His description of adolescents "going through a sort of doldrums area" in the "struggle to feel real", and as "mixture of defiance and dependence", is timeless. He points out that adolescents have a need to "prod society repeatedly so that society's antagonism is made manifest *and can be met with antagonism*" (p. 85; my emphasis).

This last observation is crucial to any analysis of the relationship between the young person and the grown-up. If antagonism is generalized and abstract, we are in serious social trouble. Donald is talking about personal, individualized antagonism in which a young person sees an adult (or a particular group) as standing up to them, as preserving their own more secure identity, in the face of protest. His use of the word "antagonism" is interesting. The dictionary defines the noun "antagonist" as "an opponent or adversary", and "antagonism" as "active opposition"; "antagonize", the verb, however, carries slightly more ambiguous definitions, first, "to counteract/neutralize" but also to "evoke hostility in, make into an enemy". Thus, these words carry an idea of adult response which is in part considered (judiciously?) as arising from established behaviours, views, and values, and in part angry, arising from the threat that the young person poses to those very behaviours, views, and values. I am sure Donald saw both. He knew that "the big challenge from the adolescent is to the bit of ourselves that has not really had its adolescence" (1965 p. 87).

Present-day official rhetoric does not use the word "antagonism" in relation to our social responses to antisocial youth. The word is much too human. We use lofty moral phrases which slightly miss the point, such as, "unacceptable behaviour" (bad) and "punishment" (sadly necessary). Note also the phrase "challenging behaviour", a silly attempt at describing young people who get up our noses without admitting to our personal feelings of antagonism.

This kind of language takes us away from the essence of Donald's argument, which seems to me to be that antisocial behaviour requires adults to contain and manage that behaviour until the young persons find ways forward which are real and meaningful to them and (and this is tough) which do not place them in self-destructive opposition to the society in which they live.

A second critical element in this approach is that it is about change through relationship. It is essentially personal. When "hopeful" opportunities arise for the child or young person to develop, it is usually the case that *someone*, that is, some person, not some establishment or organization, has been instrumental in helping that child or young person grasp the baton of hope as it is handed to them. Literacy, sport, the right job, music may be the batons of hope which are offered, but a person who cares must hand them the baton.

It is with a heavy heart that I hear and read the news today; punitive attitudes seem to prevail, whipped up by an unsavoury dialogue between some media and some leading politicians. I hope and believe that behind the rhetoric, there are constructive and hopeful interactions between the young people and those who work with them. For example, when those on Community Service orders have to wear luminous jackets, so that the general public can see that the bad guys are doing "a kind of time", there will be some working with them who will notice what they are good at or what makes them engage and respond in some way. I suppose I am longing for "goodness by stealth" at least. But the inescapable fact is that present policies and practices offer few constructive opportunities to many who are locked (literally and figuratively) into the system and all too many opportunities, through negative peer group experiences, to reinforce the behaviours which got them into trouble in the first place. There is less and less room for "personal encounters" when numbers rise and control and containment are the overriding objectives.

This is all a far cry from the provision which Donald and Clare had envisaged for children and young people in a paper on "Residential management for treatment of difficult children" (1947). A good many of the children there described, who had proved unfosterable when evacuated, would have fallen into the "antisocial" group which Clare and Donald described. Using the terminology of the war, of "hostels", Donald argued that: "[S]uccess in providing accommodation of this kind demanded residential management. It emerged, moreover, that such management in itself constituted a therapy. Further, it was important that proper management, as a therapy, should be practical; for it had to be given by relatively unskilled persons" (p. 57) (i.e., not psychotherapists but supported by such experts).

In the early days of my career, I saw for myself the remarkable work which could be done by two such persons in a local authority "hostel" for "maladjusted" children, as we called them. These people were Guy and Peggy Willatts—neither with any "relevant" experience. Various episodes stand out. Guy totally safe in the presence of some sexually provocative girls: "Put it away, dear, I've seen it all before." Having a good laugh, over gin and tonic, at the latest outrages perpetuated by the children. And Peggy, much later, widowed, old, retired, and with dementia, being looked after by a rota of some of the very same girls, now women with children, still living in the neighbourhood. I had a glimpse of "therapeutic management"; of secure adults confronting adolescents; of a response to their hopeful protests; and of being "unfazed or un-frightened" by the children, as Kahr described

Winnicott in relation to his more disturbed and vulnerable patients (2006, p. 43).

Many people of the older generations will call to mind similar people with exceptional gifts in working with children and young people in residential contexts. I am shocked when I realize how little we now refer to their work and their writing. They have vanished off the academic and professional map.

What model for youth justice?

In the last part of this paper, I want to discuss a problematic and contentious issue in youth justice policy and practice. It is one often summarized as the "welfare or justice model", but I prefer to reframe it and ask the question: "What kind of justice do antisocial young people need?" The word "welfare" has been debased. It is a fine word, meaning "satisfactory state" or "well-being". In my ethical book, justice is not being done if it has no regard to that person's well-being or "welfare".

From the 1960s onwards, our attempts to develop satisfactory policies for the treatment and management of youth offending show continuing and unresolved tensions surrounding notions of justice. This is vividly illustrated by the ideals of, and subsequent disillusionment with, the Children and Young Persons Act 1969 in Great Britain. This Act sought to elide the distinction between deprived and (put crudely) "depraved" children. It was in part based on the growing awareness of the negative effects of the bad experiences many such children had in their formative years. One practical effect of this was to be the development of interventions called "intermediate treatment" for offenders in the community. There were also to be changes in the structure of residential care. Children's homes in the local authority would be able also to admit children coming through the courts as offenders. "Approved schools" and comparable establishments were to be renamed as Community Homes with Education and might admit children who were not formally labelled as delinquent.

In the event, it all came off the rails. This was partly because there was seriously inadequate preparation and planning and staff education. Not for the first time, or the last, our legislators grossly underestimated the scale and complexity of the implementations of such a policy shift. It may have been, in fact, an impossible road to travel at that time; subsequent public reactions show the depth of hostility towards seriously antisocial youth. Those committed to these ideals ran into conflict with wider public attitudes: that phrase "bleeding heart liberals" became shorthand for people who were "soft" on the young villains, who *"explained it away"*. Furthermore, we did not know how to provide therapeutic but authoritative residential care for the diverse and highly problematic children and young people who were coming into care at an older age. Residential care in the 1970s and 1980s simply could not cope with the challenge and in some places fell into serious disrepute. The grosser aspects of this decline were found later in the scandals about sexual abuse of young people in such institutions.

In the same years, sociological evidence and theory was suggesting that a great deal of youth "crime" was simply a phase in development and best dealt with by minimum intervention (Bottoms, 2006). "Leave them alone and they'll come home." This was an attractive proposition but, even then, it seemed to me to underestimate the size and the problems of a fair number of young people, young people who would *not* pass through their "antisocial" phase without significant damage.

For some years now, the relentless focus of the media, taken up by politicians, is on the extremes of dysfunction within youth culture. It focuses on a deeply troubling segment of that culture but it seems likely that this is similarly overplayed, as was the case for "leaving them alone".

The way in which public and professional attitudes have shifted over the past fifteen years is of profound concern. Morgan and Newburn (2007, p. 1029) describe this as "the rebirth of populist punitiveness".

Of particular concern is the situation regarding custodial sentences. In a devastating critique of the current position, Morgan and Newburn make clear that, since 1998, despite the increase in non-custodial sentences, and, therefore, "a relative proportionate decline in custodial sentences", the number of children and young people sentenced to custody is "still 35% higher" than in 1998. They point out that despite reductions in reconviction rates in lower tier penalties, reconvicting from "higher tier penalties, including custody, have deteriorated from an already low base-line" (p. 1047). In short, the more severe interventions are not succeeding.

Over the years, and in many different contexts, I have found it helpful to unpack the idea of justice, using ideas from the moral philosopher Rawls (1971) and the theologian Paul Tillich (1960). Although they use different terms, they are both suggesting that there are two kinds of justice. Tillich uses the words "creative" and "proportional" to describe this. "Creative justice" is what the individual needs in order to be affirmed as a unique person; "proportional justice", implied by the word "fairness", is a recognition that we are social beings and that, to maintain social order, there have to be understandings about proportionality in respect of particular activities, good or bad.

This is well illustrated within the "good-enough" family. Good parents recognize that each child has particular likes, dislikes, needs, and capacities which require particular responses if they are to feel accepted and valued as human beings; that is, creative justice. But good parents also recognize that there are issues of "fairness" in how the family resources are shared, be it in matters of parental time, pocket money, or food. We know, of course, that notions of "fairness" peak in the latency years; in early years, the emphasis is on the need to be recognized as a unique person.

In the world of criminology and the courts, there is much talk of "the tariff", that is, the sliding scale of punishments according to the nature of the offence, without specific regard to the nature of the individual. This inevitably limits "creative justice", but, even within the tariff, discretion is exercised. A crude example would be of a group of children caught shoplifting. Who leads? Does the bigger, brighter boy require a different disposal from the one who is in a special class at school? And what kind of special factors do we take into account?

There is a curious complication when we think of this in relation to "antisocial youth". It seems to me that as we move along a continuum from "light" to "heavy" misbehaviour, the balance of justice required may move from proportional to creative. Yet I have earlier suggested that in normal development very young children need "creative" justice before proportional justice, the idea of "fair deals" kicks in later, and the balance between the two is found. It seems to me, however, that the grosser, the more violent and abusive the offences, the more likely we are to be dealing with a young person whose individual needs and feelings are so overwhelming that the notion of "fairness" has very little meaning, although it may be used as a slogan of protest. If I am right, then the case for individually focused intervention in the lives of such young people is overwhelming. Controls and punishments when rules are broken are *necessary but insufficient* if they are not related to the deeper problems and needs reflected in the gross behaviour.

What distresses me, and many others, is that since the Children and Young Persons Act 1969 (two years before Donald died), there has been little public interest in, or awareness of, the possibilities of "creative" justice as a vital element in the treatment/management of antisocial youth. Even in the world of social work, the examples which I used in my teaching have dropped away.

In contemporary practice, we have seen the separation of children's services from those of the Youth Justice Board. The role of social workers in the latter is ambiguous and reflects the distorted notion of welfare *vs.* justice. To me, it makes no sense at all to confirm in terms of a structural divide between services that "the deprived" and "the depraved" are forever to be apart. This is an opinion long held, but it has been confirmed by my work on seriously neglected children, where we see at least two different strands of service (which often do not work well together): one dealing with the gross personal deprivations of young children, another seeing the same children, a few years on, as hooligans and delinquents. This is a fundamental denial of the essentially holistic processes of development. It is nothing to do with being "soft" or "tough".

Whether we are thinking about community-based or residential interventions in the lives of antisocial youths, the element of creative justice must be present, based on an understanding of the individual, not simply the specific nature of the offences.

We have had indications of good things happening within residential care in such cases as that of Mary Bell and the boys in the Jamie Bulger case. There must have been opportunities for the building of relationships which combined both kinds of justice. What is so depressing is that, in both of those cases, unforgiving, vengeful public attitudes have threatened to scupper the work done for and with those children as they emerge into adulthood. Now we are embarking on a similar journey with the two Doncaster boys. In this case, however, I noted with interest the comment of one local resident. She said, of their neglectful family, that the younger brother, now aged ten, was, in particular, "crying out for attention from his mother and stepfather". "All they wanted was a bit of sympathy, a bit of love from their parents. For them to get into trouble, they were getting attention from their parents" (*Guardian*, 2009, p. 7).

Did the neighbour see the behaviours as carrying hope? The question must remain: Is hope extinguished or still flickering there? The importance of the quality of care now offered cannot be exaggerated. Just think of the consequences if they are failed by our services.

Nothing in Donald's writing invalidates the ideas that both of these kinds of justice are important and that the interaction of the family with the outside world is a critical factor in children's well-being. The insights from Donald's work are invaluable not least in bringing home that our responses to "antisocial youth" go to the heart of our own fear and anger at our own so called "antisocial" feelings. Increased awareness of this seems critical at this time when public manifestations of hate are at times out of control.

As usual, Donald had difficult words of wisdom and warning to say on this: "Public revenge would add up to a dangerous thing were it not for the law ... The magistrate gives expression to public revenge feelings and only by so doing can the foundations be laid for a humane treatment of the offender ... It is one of the functions of the law to protect the criminal against ... unconscious and therefore blind, revenge" (Winnicott, 1957, p. 182).

At one stroke here, Donald links the internal and the outer worlds, which is, of course, what social workers have to do.

To sum up a difficult journey:

I have tried to move between two different ways of looking at "antisocial" young persons, recognizing that the distinction which Winnicott draws between antisocial behaviour and delinquency is in practice blurred. This is partly because the antisocial behaviour is often not seen as such early enough and proceeds to delinquency—and partly because definitions of antisocial and illegal behaviour are altered by social trends and political responses. But his belief in the *meaning* of the behaviours, in particular the idea of hope, is hugely significant. The two different ways, crudely, are: first, a view of the young person as a unique individual, caught up in the family system and reacting inside and outside the family in relation to those experiences (which I think leads also to an emphasis on "creative justice"), and, second, a view of the young person as caught up in complex social forces, in particular those outside the family, which, at the very least, profoundly influence their behaviour. Many of those "forces" are concerned with forms of *inequality* and involve consideration of "proportionate justice".

I wish I could discuss all this with Donald!

References

Bottoms, A. (2006). The relationships between youth justice and child welfare in England and Wales. In: M. Hill, A. Lockyer & F. Stone (Eds.), *Youth Justice and Child Protection* (pp. 139–157). London: Jessica Kingsley.

Bowlby, J. (1951). *Maternal Care and Mental Health*. Geneva: WHO.

Children Act 1948, Geo. V1. London: H.M.S.O.

Children and Young Persons Act 1969, Eliz. II. London: H.M.S.O.

Guardian (2009). Doncaster torture case: Social workers should have intervened sooner. 4 September, p. 7.

Hollin, C. (2007). Criminological psychology. In: M. Macquire, R. Morgan & R. Reiner (Eds.), *The Oxford Handbook of Criminology* (4th edn). Oxford: Oxford University Press.

Kahr, B. (2006). Winnicott's contribution to the study of dangerousness. In: R. Morgan & S. Hollins (Eds.), *Young People and Crime* (pp. 39–45). London: Karnac.

Morgan, R. & Newburn, T. (2007). Youth justice. In: M. Macquire, R. Morgan & R. Reiner (Eds.), *The Oxford Handbook of Criminology*. Oxford: Oxford University Press.

Pitts, J. (2008). *Reluctant Gangsters: The Changing Face of Youth Crime*. Cullompton: Willan Publishing.

Rawls, J. (1971). *A Theory of Justice*. Harvard: Harvard University Press.

Robertson, J. (1953). *Film: A Two-year-old Goes to Hospital*. 16 mm. Ipswich: Concord Films.

Robertson, J., Bowlby, J. &, Rosenblatt, D. (1952). Responses of young children to separation from their mothers. In: *Psychoanalytic Study of the Child* (Vol. 7) (pp. 82–94). London: Imago.

Rutter, M., Beckett, C., Castle, J., Kreppner, J., Stevens, S. & Sonuga-Barke, E. (2009). *Policy and Practice Implications from the English and Romanian Adoptees (ERA) Study: 45 Key Questions*. London: BAAF.

Stevenson, O. (2007). *Neglected Children and Their Families*. Oxford: Blackwell.

Tillich, P. (1960). *Love, Power and Justice*. Oxford: Oxford University Press.

Wilkinson, R. & Pickett, K. (2009). *The Spirit Level*. London: Allen & Unwin.

Winnicott, D. W. (1956). The Antisocial Tendency. In: *Collected Papers: Through Paediatrics to Psycho-Analysis* (pp. 306–315). London: Tavistock.

Winnicott D. W. (1957). *The Child and the Outside World*. London: Tavistock.

Winnicott, D. W. (1965). Adolescence: struggling through the doldrums. In: *The Family and Individual Development* (pp. 79–87). London: Tavistock.

Winnicott, D. W. (1986). Delinquency as a sign of hope. In: C. Winnicott, R. Shepherd & M. Davis (Eds.), *Home is Where We Start From* (pp. 90–100). London: Penguin.

Winnicott, D. W. & Britton, C. (1947). Residential management as a treatment for difficult children. In: C. Winnicott, R. Shepherd & M. Davis (Eds.), *Deprivation and Delinquency* (pp. 54–72). London: Tavistock Publications.

Can the state ever be a "good-enough parent"?

Christopher Reeves

The family and the state: an uncertain compact

My starting point is a commonplace. It is this: In British society there currently exists a pervasive unease over children and their upbringing, especially the more marginalized and vulnerable young people in society. This unease encompasses both what "wayward youth" inflicts on society, and what certain adults in society, parents or carers, perversely visit on small and defenceless children. It is not new, but the anxiety invested in it is. It registers in the shocked reaction to the recent phenomenon of teenage gangs rampaging and causing damage in city centres, acting as if apparently quite independent of, or oblivious to, parental controls; and also in revulsion at widely publicized cases of child abuse. Here, the recent tragic case of Baby Peter continues to resonate in the public mind.

In this lecture, I shall be addressing this last mentioned area of public concern, where the child or young person is seen as victim, not as victimizer. Other contributors in this series will be concerned with the phenomenon and challenge of "wayward youth".

I have mentioned Baby Peter as emblematic of the perceived failings of society in regard to abused or neglected children. You will doubtless recall how the previous comparable major Child Protection failure—that of the death of five year-old Victoria Climbié at the hands of family minders, begot a raft of new legislation culminating in the government's Every Child Matters initiative. These enactments, it was hoped, would put an end to the series of child care disasters of the previous forty years by requiring services to be focused squarely on the child as a person in need and potentially at risk. Yet in spite of all this, just a few years later here with Baby Peter was yet another instance of a child that appeared not to matter enough simply as *a child*, but rather as *a factor*, a case on somebody's caseload, or the subject of a child protection conference. In the process, the reality and the urgency of his predicament got lost. What made matters worse of course was that Baby Peter's safeguarding was the responsibility of the same local authority that had so dismally failed Victoria Climbié on the previous occasion. Even worse, once the tragedy unfolded, much of the authority's efforts appeared to be directed at fending off criticism of its actions. All of this served to underline in the mind of the public the extent to which the concerns of professionals seemingly took precedence over those of the children they were supposed to be caring for. How, it was asked, could matters have come to such a pass?

The public unease I refer to is compounded, I believe, by an underlying mood of despair at the recurrence of such instances and by our apparent inability as a society to put them right and prevent them from happening in the future. Faced with the reality, two sorts of response are possible. The first, favoured by government, is to particularize each event, lambasting those individuals identified as being responsible for the debacle, while laying down ever-stricter guidelines to ensure that it will not and cannot happen again. The second, more reflective and less purely reactive response, is to countenance one's personal sense of disbelief and question why these tragedies occur, not instance by instance—considering each as a distinct phenomenon with a discreet causation—but as a seeming series, yet at the same time striking us as individually determined occurrences, each one shocking, surprising, and inexplicable.

The question is, are we right to be surprised? Or could our feeling of incredulity be linked to a generalized denial mechanism, a social compact, unwittingly, but not unwilfully, to overlook something potentially obvious about the way we *care for* children, as distinct from being *concerned about* them? Being concerned in a sentimental fashion does not cost much; it can be intermittent, a matter of attitude rather than action. But is the price of proper caring, in personal, social, financial, and political terms, more perhaps than as a society we are prepared to pay? It involves continuity, sustained involvement, and investment. Needless to say, this second sort of soul-searching response has not been much in evidence in the wake of the Baby Peter affair. It is easier to allocate blame than to analyse dispassionately what might be going wrong at the level of society, and what might be needed in order to put it right.

As a preliminary to such an analysis, I want to point to a number of underlying features in current public policy over the care of children. First, caring is treated as virtually tantamount to keeping them safe—or at least this trumps every other consideration. Second, there is a manifest polarization of attitudes in the public about how children should be safeguarded. People take sides, not about the ultimate aim of ensuring their well-being, but about the best way of doing so. Some argue in favour of removing children at the first indication of risk. Others point to the deleterious effects of separating children from their birth parents. Third, even when an individual in an official capacity and charged with determining what action to take, or what policy to pursue, makes a pronouncement about what should happen, be it a government minister, an adviser, politician, or head of children's services, each is relying ultimately on their personal experience of upbringing in judging what needs to be done. These are not at root political decisions (although political factors may influence them), nor are they based on specialized economic, business, anthropological, or even psychological knowledge about the management of people. No, they derive from ideas and experience about children, parenting, and family life that are common to most adults in society. It is because their critics also have, or assume, a comparable experience, that such decisions are peculiarly susceptible to challenge, especially in a climate of uncertainty and disarray. It is like an argument between parents over how to manage an unruly child. Sounds of mutual scolding and recrimination rend the air, and along with it an insistence that one view or course of action has to prevail: *You may think that, but I think this!* In such circumstances the dominant voice prevails; the other is left sullen and unconvinced.

I suggest that the reasons as to why in these matters different considerations or imperatives so often appear to collide without any apparent room for dialogue and compromise, is because underlying them is a flight from an uncomfortable reality that is at once straightforward and challenging. What is simple is the self-evident truth that children need parents, and parenting involves partnership, sharing. I don't mean just the fact of the sharing of parenthood, but the sharing of relationships, parent-to-parent, parent-to-child, child-to-parent. What is difficult is the intrinsic triangularity of family relationships and the resulting dissonance, as well as the consonance, this engenders. It means that parents often fail their children when dissonance leads to conflict, and conflict to entrenched opposition. Many separations and divorces are effected through the desire of one parent or both to protect the child(ren) from the consequences of such opposition and conflict—to preserve a measure of consonance. Yet even with only one parent present and actively caring for the child, the parental function remains triangulated: the mother, say, in her role of nurturer required to be at once facilitator and boundary-setter. And the alternative, the deliberate avoidance of confrontation at all costs, can easily lead to a collusive pseudo-companionship between adult and child that risks interrupting or distorting the maturational process as much as inter-parental conflict did or would.

Let me turn the focus back now from the child and family, to the "outer world", the point where we started. When family nurturant functions are, for whatever reason, tendered out for an indefinite period—when children become "other people's children" for whatever reason—I argue that this element of triangularity tends to travel with them. So too, and even more strongly than in the actual single parent family, does the tendency to seek to mitigate the potential for conflict-generating measures, or to embrace strategies of care designed not necessarily in the best interests of the child, but of oneself as parent, or parent-proxy, thereby turning the threesome into a twosome. In social work, terminating or restricting access to the other parent—circumscribing access in order supposedly to prevent distress and disruption for the child in care, in reality to make the expression of that distress more copable with by the adult—is a decision often constituting a flight from triangularity. And of course, the same applies to the current temptation in the wake of high-profile safeguarding failures for children's service departments as a whole to remove children at risk from families and place them in care, as a self safeguarding measure rather than a child safeguarding one. A twosome is easier to deal with than a threesome.

Wartime evacuation and the growing recognition of the state's obligation towards the child

I want now to situate these observations in a still wider context. I have adapted the title of this talk from the chapter heading "The state as a parent" in Stephen Cretney's thought-provoking book *Law, Law Reform and the Family* (1998). In the chapter in question Cretney considered the coming into being of the Children Act 1948 and the events leading up to it. He rightly viewed this Act as one of the most significant and far-reaching pieces of legislation, not just in the context of the post-war Atlee government's establishment of the Welfare State, but in defining the wider relationship between government and the governed, the State and the individual, for the next half century and beyond.

Briefly, what the Children Act sought to do was (I quote): "provide a comprehensive service for the care of children deprived of the benefit of a normal home life" (1948, Cmd. 7306, para. 1).

So accustomed have we become to expect and experience the State legislating on behalf of the welfare of children in virtually every aspect of their lives, that it requires a real effort to envisage the actual situation prevailing in British society before the publication of the Beveridge Report on the future Welfare State over sixty-five years ago. Then, central government had no more than a monitoring role in respect of the care of children deprived of family life, and formally speaking, none at all, save in exceptional circumstances, in respect of the welfare, upbringing, and moral education of children brought up within their own families or by relatives. Up to that time, the statutory care of children deprived of family life was wholly vested in local authorities according to the terms of the Poor Law Act 1930.

This Act was itself a carryover in many respects from the Elizabethan provisions of 1603 that had required local communities to provide workhouses and for the children housed there to be prepared for service, in the case of girls, and manual work, in the case of boys. Of course this Dickensian (in fact, pre-Dickensian) picture of children prematurely put out to labour had changed somewhat during the Victorian era owing to the establishment of large organizations such as Barnado's and the National Children's Home, each providing, from voluntary contributions, for the needs of orphans. Most of these were church-based and had a larger vision of what preparation for a life of work entailed, but were not funded, licensed, or regulated by the State. This was because the care of children, in terms of their physical, social, and moral welfare, was not deemed to be the proper business of government. While the 1930 Act had introduced as an alternative to the workhouse or institutional upbringing an idea of "boarding out" or "billeting"—the latter term in particular carrying with it wartime associations of individuals foisted on to reluctant families—still absent was any concept of a deprived child's entitlement to something better than ceasing to be an economic burden to the community at the earliest possible opportunity.

The 1938–1939 Evacuation programme changed all that. This was the first occasion in British history that the State undertook a course of action directly aimed at protecting its young citizens and ensuring their welfare over the heads of their parents, in short, taking on a pro-parental role. Since parents as a whole could not protect their children from blanket bombing, it was incumbent on the State to act on their behalf. The evacuation exercise in wartime, along with some of its unintended consequences, constituted one major factor in the chain of events that lead up to the passing of the Children Act 1948. For what became apparent was that there were secondary, psychological consequences to removing children from the care of their parents—consequences that had been flagged up by Winnicott, Bowlby, and Emmanuel Miller at the outset of the operation.

Unsurprisingly to them (although it was not generally anticipated by the public and by politicians at the time), many children reacted adversely to their enforced separation from their parents. It was not a case of them just becoming upset—that was predictable—but—and this was not seen as predictable—they became actively upsetting as well. Moreover, when this sort of thing happened on a relatively large scale across the country, wherever children were billeted, the ensuing emotional and behavioural problems could not just be left to individual parents or the host community to deal with as in the past. Services had to be put in place to manage the psychological problems that evacuation had given rise to. Here the findings of the Cambridge Evacuation Survey (1941), undertaken by Susan Isaacs, and the report of Winnicott and Clare Britton (1947)—as she then was—based on their collaborative experience with the evacuation hostels in Oxfordshire, provided invaluable evidence for government of what was needed and could be done. In addition, at the end of the war there remained a significant number of children—at least as many as the total pre-war number of children in need of Public Assistance provision—who could not be returned to their parents with the expectation of family life carrying on as normal. This was because their parents were dead, or out of contact, or unwilling to take their children back, or the children themselves were by now too unmanageable to be absorbed back into their families without more ado. So it fell to the central government, having in a sense created the problem through its proxy-parenting initiative, to find the means of resolving it.

The aftermath of evacuation was one factor, but by no means the only one, in the sequence of events leading towards the Children Act 1948. There was a strong ideological impulse in play as well. War proved a great leveller. Bombing and the ruin of homes affected rich and poor alike. The fighting and the departure of fathers to the front for years on end were universal experiences for families. All shared the burden, and the great imperative of the post-war administration and the setting up of the Welfare State was that all should share the benefits of victory. So, in the case of children's social welfare, just as in the case of health and education, no longer was there to be one provision for the advantaged and another for the disadvantaged. Providing a "comprehensive service for the care of children deprived of the benefit of normal family life", as the Children Act 1948 proclaimed in its preamble, meant ensuring as far as possible the same opportunities of education and advancement, and importantly the same "quality of life".

And then, as if to emphasize the urgent need for change, there occurred in January 1945 the appalling death in care of a twelve year-old, Dennis O'Neill, as a result of sustained physical abuse and starvation, when he and his brother had been "billeted out" with unsupervised foster carers on a remote Shropshire farm. The ensuing government inquiry catalogued a litany of mismanagement, poor communication, and lack of liaison between those responsible for the care of the boys. For the first, but not by any means the last, time, the public cry went out: "*This sort of thing must never be allowed to happen again.*" The impetus for change had become irresistible.

Winnicott and the implications of the state's "duty to care"

But what did this new undertaking of providing a comprehensive service for children deprived of normal family life mean in practice, in terms of government responsibility? Did it mean, as Cretney suggests, that the State thenceforward took on, and saw itself as taking on, a quasi-parental role? When I discussed the significance of the Children Act 1948 and the Curtis Report that preceded it in a chapter for Judith Issroff's book *Donald Winnicott and John Bowlby: Personal and Professional Perspectives* (Reeves, 2006a, pp. 179–207), I suggested that what central government implicitly accepted at this juncture was "a duty to care", and that specifically towards young people in need. What by Elizabethan legislation had been made a *de facto* duty to care vested in the local community, and had then in 1930 passed to local government, was now being taken over by central government.

This "duty to care" had three aspects or components. First, it was preventive, in that it sought to remove children from abuse or neglect—what we nowadays term, legalistically, as discharging a "duty *of* care". Second, it provided resources for the proper caring of those in need of care. Third, it enabled, by means of legislation, a framework to be put in place that would ensure that this function of caring was put into practice and monitored. However—and this is a point worth underlining—it did not at this stage mean government being directly responsible for the actual care of children in need, hence answerable for its quality and what is nowadays termed its "delivery". That was a matter for the professionals commissioned by local authorities to ensure, the new Children's Officers, whose task would be, in the words of the Act, "to further the child's best interests, and to afford him opportunity for the proper development of his character and abilities" (Children Act 1948, Section 12(1)).

I have so far made a couple of passing references to Winnicott. It is now time to draw him into the centre of the picture, because he was both involved and preoccupied with this particular phase of British social history and his reflections on it bear scrutiny, even now. Referring to the Children Act 1948 as "preventive medicine in respect of delinquency" he suggested that "perhaps the most positive use made by society of psychoanalytic findings has been in the approach to the problems of antisocial behaviour" (Winnicott, 1986, p. 181).

Undoubtedly, one point of difference about the Children Act 1948 from the series of subsequent Children Acts that have punctuated the following sixty years, is that neither the government of the day, nor the Committee convened to advise it on legislation (the Curtis Committee), actually considered itself as already having substantive answers to the issues on which legislation was proposed. It being a new departure, government ministers at the time were genuinely in search of advice and direction. To this end, they naturally turned to those they regarded as experts in the field. Winnicott was one such presumed authority. In fact, he was one of no less than four present or future psychoanalysts called to give evidence before the Curtis Committee (the others being John Bowlby, Susan Isaacs, and Clare Britton). I think this must be a unique occurrence in British legislative history.

Winnicott's public credentials had become well established through his series of wartime broadcasts intended for parents who were having to come to terms with separation from their evacuated children. Meanwhile, his practical knowledge of the realities of the evacuation experience for the children concerned and for those having the unsolicited task of looking after them had been acquired through his weekly sorties to Oxfordshire to visit and advise the staff of a series of hostels set up to house the more unbiddable and unbillatable among them. During this period, the emotional problems of these children and what he came to call the "nuisance value" of their symptomatic reactions to separation, caused him to radically reappraise his earlier beliefs about the psychogenesis of antisocial behaviour. Whereas pre-war he was among the majority of psychoanalysts viewing environmental factors (by which was meant "real-life experiences") as at best incidental contributors to psychological disturbance when compared with internal drive factors, by its end he was firmly on Bowlby's side in insisting on the importance of understanding the impact of life events on the dispositions of young people.

However, Winnicott and Bowlby were not in full accord in the evidence each presented to the Curtis Committee (Reeves, 2006b). While both emphasized the injurious effects of separating children from their families, Bowlby's view was that, wherever possible, recovery could only be brought about by reintegrating the child into the family at the earliest possible moment, or failing that, by attaching him or her to another family that would become a real, life-long substitute for the original one. Better a less than adequate home than an institution, however caring, was Bowlby's recommendation.

Winnicott did not wholly agree with this. His starting point was that the psychological effects of separation were akin to an illness that needed to be addressed by a programme of remedial action. What this meant in practice is that while home was where the restored child should return to, it was not necessarily the ideal setting in which to effect the cure. It was not ideal if the "illness", so to speak, had really taken hold, or if the child had not already established an initial trusting relationship to their parents before they had been removed. What such children needed first and foremost was what he called "primary home experience", that is to say, an intensive provision of the sort of minute-by-minute unconditional adaptation to need that should ideally have been supplied at the start of life. This retrospective therapeutic input, he argued, could best be supplied in specially adapted residential environments. To this end, he was in favour of maintaining the existing hostels after the evacuation emergency was over, whereas Bowlby was in favour of closing them down.

It can be seen then that Winnicott was wholeheartedly behind the impetus of government as part of its strategy for the Welfare State to ensure that all children deprived of family life should be provided for appropriately in terms of their psychological as well as social and educational well-being. At the same time, he was strongly against State interference in health and welfare functions for its own sake, as is clear from a rather intemperate letter he wrote to Lord Beveridge on the subject of the National Health Service at the time. As he saw it, the new health service provisions would mean that doctors would in future become just another branch of the Civil Service.

What are we to make of Winnicott's overall attitude towards the Beveridge-inspired project for welfare reform in general—its democratic aspect—and, in particular, its future provisions for children in need? How to reconcile his demand that professionals—in this case, doctors—should be left to get on with their work unconstrained by government with his evident desire that State-sponsored residential care should be provided where necessary for therapeutically treating the sorts of emotional and behavioural difficulties of children, through what he termed "management", when they could not be dealt with in a foster family context? Is there an inconsistency between his advocacy of a *laissez-faire* policy in the first case, and recommending government intervention in the other?

I want now to show that there wasn't, and this can best be done by examining more closely why it was that both Winnicott and Clare Britton wholeheartedly supported the provisions of the Children Act 1948. Indeed, one might even go so far as to say that they were among its principal architects, since the evidence they jointly presented to the Curtis Committee proved crucial in fashioning one of the key enactments of the subsequent legislation. This was the requirement that each new local authority children's service should have at its head a Children's Officer charged with knowing in a personal way all the children in that authority's care. Here Clare Britton's example and the legacy from the Oxfordshire evacuation scheme are clearly in evidence.

When quizzed by Myra Curtis, she had been adamant that her situation and responsibilities in the conditions of wartime could be replicated in the new order. She argued that it was not beyond the capability of any person of the calibre required of a Children's Officer to have the necessary personal knowledge and investment, provided only that the supporting structure of the local authority was an enabling one. Therefore, in the ensuing legislation it was enjoined that the organizational and managerial requirements of the post of Children's Officer should not get in the way of this primary personal responsibility for the children in her care.

The key element I want to pick out here is that the Children's Officer was intended to be a practitioner primarily, rather than a manager. I use the term "practitioner" advisedly, because of its association with the established term "General Practitioner" for the family doctor. What Winnicott, I think, valued, about the role of the General Practitioner, was his personal knowledge of and responsibility for his patient list. Knowledge, responsibility, and efficacy went hand in hand. And this is what he saw, rightly or wrongly, as being under threat due to the government's proposed institution of the National Health Service. His argument was not that the government should not do its utmost to facilitate equal access for all to medical care. It was rather that the government should not needlessly intervene in the relationship between doctor (the "practitioner") and patient. If individual doctors were performing their duties satisfactorily, then there was no need for governmental intrusion.

A similar rubric was to be applied to the proposed Children's Officers, at least in the minds of Clare and Donald Winnicott. Establish the structure within which the role can be discharged for each local authority, and then leave it to the person appointed to function as best she can (it was generally assumed that the Children's Officer would be a woman). Underpinning this conviction that the practitioner should always be enabled to practise and as far as possible left to it, was something quite fundamental to Winnicott's view of good functioning, and therefore of good governance. It revolved around his ideas about process and environment and the facilitation of one by the other in the interests of *creative responding* and derived from his thoughts about the family nexus. At its root lay the vision of the mother's facilitation of the baby's earliest maturation, where the mother provides cover, a sort of emotional womb for the not-yet-I, not "fledged", infant.

Yet such of course is by no means a static or stable condition in Winnicott's view. The outer shell provides a protection, yet at the same time it is something that has eventually to be pierced from within, passed out of and beyond; and this, ultimately, in the interest of the growing child's capacity for creative living. Therefore, there is a paradox here; protection by the protective screen and the push to overmaster it are equipoized: the twin tendencies are in a state of dynamic tension. Winnicott's particular insight was to grasp that this necessary tension was both enabled and sustained by the presence of the third figure, conventionally represented by the father. He it was who ideally constituted an outer protective screen, like a skin to this dynamic facilitating environment of the mother–infant dyad. The analogy he used was borrowed straight from Freud, albeit put to use in a different context. It was that of the protective membrane, or the "shield against stimuli" (Winnicott, 1965, p. 147). The father protects the dyad in the way that the mother protects the baby. And just as that maternal protective layer must allowably be pierced from time to time if further growth is to occur, so the outer shield must be susceptible to impingements. That is, the outer world with its requirements and constraints must sometimes impact on the family—"seep in" was Winnicott's term—if the child is in due course to mature and grow outwards, beyond the confines of the nurturing family. The mother must be "good enough", not perfect, the family left as far as possible to be a "going concern".

Transposing this from the micro to the macro level, the worst thing a government can do, in Winnicott's eyes, is to interfere with a properly functioning family unit. However, old-style government non-intervention is not the answer either, the reason being that there is no guarantee that the "field of force" that is the family dynamic will remain stable, self-sufficient, and self-supporting, any more than maternal care will always be enabling and ideally adaptive. Being "good enough" in Winnicott's terms means on occasion being allowed to be bad enough to fail, and then to recover and remedy the deficit. It is just here, at points of crisis or potential failure, that the figure of the third, the outer protective cover for the inner system, is called on to intervene. Primarily, Winnicott had in mind the father in relation to the mother and child. However, he applied exactly the same line of reasoning within a sociological perspective in regard to the outer layer supplied by the social system, namely, the community that surrounds and contextualizes the family.

From this perspective, the social network, both informal and formal, is seen as being a necessary adjunct at certain times for the individual family in order for it to deal with the latent "antisocial tendencies" that are part of the process of the child's growing up to adolescence and beyond. This need for community "cover" applies to the family that is a "going concern" and crucially to ones where, for whatever reason, "the antisocial tendency", a by-product of deprivation, has taken hold and is threatening to become organized into delinquent acting-out.

The state as protective membrane for the family

So, on Winnicott's premises, government is wrong routinely to interfere with the family as a going concern; and equally remiss if it fails to provide a network supporting environment for the struggling family. The question is: What sort of support must it provide? Or to put it in other terms, what sort of higher order parenting is required of the State? At this point I am going to plead your indulgence in referring to different sorts of protective function, as the maternal and paternal respectively. In doing so I am trying to replicate the contours of Winnicott's own thinking as faithfully I can, at the same time as being aware, as he would surely have been, of the transitive nature of the terms themselves in changing times, and of the ultimately indeterminate relationship with the actual gender of the figures on whom they are predicated. However, it is clear that Winnicott regarded the triangularly of the family as absolutely intrinsic both in terms of its authentic structure and its perennial functioning. So I intend to go on using the terms "maternal" and "paternal" on licence as it were, to distinguish the complementary caring functions that are protective of the unit within—in the first instance of course having the infant at its centre—and afterwards the mother–child dyad, and then the family as a unit in relation to the "outer world". In each case the outer, or what I term "the paternal function", denotes the facilitating environment in relation to which that unit responds and reacts. It is clear according to this analysis, therefore, that in Winnicott's eyes, the State was primarily an inheritor of the father's role in regard to the family unit.

The clearest way in which Winnicott ascribes a largely benign paternal function exercised (or exercisable) by society as a whole in relation to the family is in regard to "law"—what we nowadays tend to bracket as "law and order". He postulated this as the "indestructible environment" against which the young person's rebelliousness eventually flounders—not in vain, and hopelessly, but constructively. It is a case—at a higher order if you like—of the sort of *realization* (a favourite term of his) of the subjective world encountering the objective world objectively perceived. This happens (I am talking about the constructive case) when the provocation of, say, the adolescent testing and transgressing family boundaries through antisocial behaviour is met no longer simply by parental sanctions that are now experienced by the young person as unavailing, but by the impersonality of the magistracy. The formal, judicial nature of the confrontation is part of its strength; if you like, of its therapeutic potential. This is because the quasi-magical component of the conflict that initially contributed to the delinquent act, arising out of conflict, provocation, and challenge within the family unit, is here detoxified by the emotional detachment of the legal process itself. That the representatives of public authority, police, magistrates, politicians, and behind them, the Home Secretary of the day, are not personally provoked, do not feel personally challenged by the young person's behaviour, is an important factor, both in helping the individual to experience the security of a boundary to their capacity to challenge, and for the parents themselves in coming to recognize the necessary limits to their authority, that is to say, to their capacity to contain and restrain, however galling that may be for them. This, at least, was Winnicott's ascription of the benign function of law.

I shall comment further on how matters have changed in this sphere since Winnicott's day, and the implications of this change, at the conclusion of my lecture. At this juncture, I want to point out that Winnicott was opposed to magistrates regarding themselves in a therapeutic role. That magistrates should care about the juveniles who came before them was fine, that they should seek to reform them through care management was not. The job of magistrates was to acknowledge the actual provocation implicit within the "nuisance value" of the delinquent act and to punish it, thereby giving expression in a contained way to the revenge feelings of society, its hatred towards the offender—in short, its "taking offence". Winnicott was impatient with the denial of the provocative intention. Delinquency might be a sign of "hope", but it was equally a sign of hate and had to be acknowledged as such. I imagine that he would have regarded the frequently used modern phrase "challenging behaviour" with some disdain, since it falsely appears to suggest that antisocial acts are managerially problematic rather than provoking for the adults who have to confront and deal with them. "Challenging behaviour" diminishes the person of the offender, rendering his or her motivation, its "nuisance value", as being of little consequence. It is treated as challenging for, rather than challenging to, the grown-ups. The danger of this shift is that if the vengeful feelings of the young person go unacknowledged, and also the revenge feelings of society, sentimental attitudes are likely to prevail, with the consequent risk of those holding on to such attitudes visiting unconscious hatred on the youthful perpetrators under the guise of benevolently intentioned behaviour.

All this emphasis on punishment may seem rather harsh, and difficult to reconcile with the essentially caring and restitutive figure of Winnicott we think we know. Yet the fact is that Winnicott did believe in punishment and not only in the judicial context, but also in the right of those caring for children physically to punish those for whom they were responsible. He argued in favour of this before the Curtis Committee (and earned strong criticism from fellow analyst Edward Glover for doing so), although on this matter the Committee did not follow his advice and instead recommended the prohibition of all forms of corporal punishment of children, at least in foster placements and in ordinary care homes. Was Winnicott just unenlightened, perhaps conditioned, by his own schoolboy culture? Whether one disagrees with Winnicott in this particular, as I imagine most would nowadays, I think it is important to recognize the underlying paradigm that led him to adopt this position. It is a matter once more of referring back to the container and the contained, or in Winnicott's terms, to "the maturational process" and "the facilitating environment", and in furtherance of that, to the complementary roles of mother and father. For Winnicott, the father should above all be "strict and strong", an antidote not to the ineffectual mother, but to the mother as still in important respects a "subjective object" for the child. The father represents the "objectivity" of the external world. Of his own father, Winnicott remarked late on that "perhaps he left me too much to mothers"—meaning to his own detriment. In embracing the guiding premise of the Children Act 1948, therefore, namely, to provide a *comprehensive* service for children deprived of normal family life, Winnicott was strongly of the opinion that, on the one hand, such children should not be left too much to "fathers" (as I suspect he felt had been the case with the punitive and controlling nature of too much institutional care up to then), nor yet to the exclusive care of "mothers".

Thus he was in favour of government oversight of the new provisions being transferred from the Home Office to Health because of the association of the former with the penal system and Borstals (although this didn't actually happen for another twenty years). At the same time he argued in favour of having couples—ideally man and wife—running the new family group homes. If overdosing on fathers led to the creation of rigid, over-controlled, or punitive characters, or reactively turned them towards membership of delinquent gangs, overdosing on mothers could lead to children leaving care as dependent individuals, over-compliant, uncreative, and immature or else, in reaction, as precociously independent ones, where the appearance of maturity was liable to give way eventually to depressive illness and incapacity to cope, especially when faced with responsibility for their own children—the syndrome later known as "the cycle of deprivation".

The ultimate function of the family in Winnicott's view was to enhance the child's creativity, spontaneity, and maturity. It depended on the triangular relationship at its core, where the roles of the parents were by turns those of "covering" and "being covered", of contrast, complementarity, and collaboration. And when Winnicott envisaged the remit for those entrusted with the care of the deprived child by the terms of the Children Act 1948, to provide as far as possible the advantages of a normal family upbringing, the enhancement of creativity, spontaneity, and mature independence were as important for the child as were his or her physical, educational, and social well-being. Hence, Winnicott's stress on the essentially practitioner role of the caregivers, complemented by the support of the organizational managers. Practitioners were to be given the freedom to do their job according to their own professional instincts, albeit with the encouragement, advice, and only intermittently the direction of those in a consultative or management relationship to them.

The dismantling of the children's service: Seebohm and after

By and large, this was the pattern of care that unfolded over the twenty years following the implementation of the Children Act 1948. Many who recall this period, particularly those who were Children's Officers at the time, as well as the Winnicotts themselves, lamented the organizational changes set in train by the 1968 Seebohm Report, while recognizing and in part supporting the impetus that prompted it, to achieve better co-ordination of the support and welfare services available for deprived children and their families. What was lost as a result of these later changes was not only the dedicated role of the Children's Officer in each local authority, but with it the central concept of the personal practitioner service to the individual child, of which the institution of the Children's Officer role has been seen as an embodiment and guarantor (Heywood, 1978).

To highlight the consequences of this loss, one need point to just one fact. Whereas in the quarter century following the death in care of Dennis O'Neill no major government inquiries took place into the death of children in care, in the following quarter century there was a succession of them, beginning with the Maria Colwell Inquiry of 1974, then the Jasmine Beckford Inquiry of 1985, and then the Kimberly Carlile Inquiry of 1987, the Rikki Neave Inquiry of 1994, the Victoria Climbié Inquiry of 2003, and most recently the Baby Peter Inquiry of 2009. And these are only the best known ones. A recent Community Care article catalogued more than twenty such inquiries over these years. Of course, in the process the system of child care has been reformed and revamped, with the aim of improving the quality of care provided. So, the Colwell Inquiry focused on the need for better inter-agency communication (itself a major contributor, incidentally, to the death of Dennis O'Neill thirty years earlier). To meet this deficiency, the subsequent Children Act 1975 concentrated on instituting better systems of communications for children at risk, notably, the Child Protection Review. Note, however, that in the course of this the primacy of the practitioner process has given way to the primacy of procedure-based practice. One is open-ended and interrogative, the other aim-directed and structured. "Good" social workers were no longer principally identified by the quality of their contact and communication with the child, and their assessments based on this, but by their efficiency in ensuring that the correct procedures of assessment and liaison were instituted and their conclusions carried through. Quarter of a century on, the Victoria Climbié Inquiry in its turn inaugurated a new era in which protocols began to take precedence over professional procedures. Now what was most important was that professionals should record, and then transmit, information. (I haven't used the word "communicated" because this implies an active reciprocity between giver and receiver, the active sharing of information; recording data on a database in the expectation that it will be retrieved in due course does not.)

Following the publication of the Climbié Report but antedating the latest child care tragedy, the child care expert Professor Nigel Parton (2004, pp. 80–94) suggested that one of the factors that stood out from his analysis of the succession of inquiries from 1970 onwards is that the solutions proposed and the measures instituted following the last inquiry seem often to emerge as principal contributory factors in precipitating the next catastrophe. He highlighted in particular the growth of what he calls "managerialization" and "audit" in the care services and the consequent downgrading of what I refer to as the role of *"practitioner process"*. The growth of these two factors, managerialization and audit, are of course not unique to social services, but I want to confine my remarks to this field.

The usual way of explaining this growth has been to point to the increased complexity of the field over the past sixty years, due among other things to the fact that the remit for the provision of care services is no longer so narrowly defined in terms of children deprived of family life, but extends potentially to all children in society ("Every Child Matters"); to the fact too that families, not just the children, are encompassed by the provisions for safeguarding; to the fact that the profile of the two-parent family, where both adults are usually the parents of each and all of the children, is no longer the norm, perhaps not even the standard model in identifying support structures and targeting services; and lastly to the fact that globalization and multi-ethnicity have led in many areas to a proliferation of looser groupings that all call themselves, or can be identified as, in some sense the "family" but at one time would not have been treated as such. This phenomenon of the increasingly fluid nature of family groupings, especially in certain areas of the country, was a factor strongly in evidence in the two latest inquiries.

But complexity is not enough in itself to explain the transformation, some would say, the degradation, of services designed to promote the care of children in the widest sense over the past forty years. Something more fundamental seems to have gone wrong. But what exactly?

In search of an answer I want to return to Winnicott, but do so first by way of a one-time student of Winnicott and the preceding lecturer in this series, Professor Olive Stevenson. Among her many important posts and responsibilities in the field of Social Work policy and practice, she was a member of a Commission appointed by the government in 1974 to report on the Maria Colwell case. Perhaps uniquely in the history of these public inquiries into high-profile deaths of children in care, she elected at its conclusion to submit a minority report, dissociating herself from some of the findings of the other panel members. I want to quote you a relevant passage of her own report, one picked up by Professor Parton in the lecture I referred to earlier:

> The overall impression created by Maria's sad history is that while individuals made mistakes it was "the system", using the word in the widest sense, that failed her. Because that system is the product of society it is upon society as a whole that the ultimate blame must rest. Indeed, the highly emotional and angry reaction of the public in this case indicates society's troubled conscience. It is not enough for the state as representing society to assume responsibility for those such as Maria. It must also provide the means to do so, both financially and by ensuring that the system works as efficiently as possible at every level so that individual mistakes which must be accepted as inevitable, do not result in disaster.
>
> (Parton, 2004, p. 90)

Olive Stevenson is appealing here to two fundamental tenets of Winnicott. The first is that "good-enough mothering" includes the acceptance of occasional inevitable, but rectifiable, failures (Winnicott, 1962, p. 57). The second is that preventing such failures from turning into disasters—in the case of the baby into a failure of "going on being"; in the older child, of neglect, abandonment, and possibly death—depends upon the secure provision of an outer facilitating environment, loosely identified with the paternal (Winnicott, 1960, p. 90), which by its considered, constructive, and sometimes critical support, promotes and preserves the conditions of good-enough maternal functioning (in the present context this being identifiable with the social worker's practitioner process).

The "oppressive boundary": the over-intrusive state

Too easily this facilitating boundary can get replaced by what Davis and Wallbridge (1981, p. 151) in their excellent account of Winnicottian theory call "the oppressive boundary". This comes about when the family boundary is fractured, primarily through the absence or ineffectualness of the father, whereupon, instead of intervening facilitatively, only when and as necessary, a type of external intervention occurs that insufficiently respects and supports the family's ability to reconstitute and carry on. About this danger, Winnicott (1964, p. 171) was categorical, writing: "Whatever does not specifically back up the idea that parents are responsible people will in the long run be very harmful to the core of society."

Among the impingements—what he termed the "common persecutions"—that he saw the poor and more vulnerable members of society exposed to, he listed "overcrowding, starvation, infestation" and "the constant threat of physical disease and disaster" as well as *"the laws promulgated by a benevolent society"* (Winnicott, 1968, p. 155; my emphasis).

One last recurrent Winnicott theme I want to mention here. I have referred intermittently to his idea of the threesome, the triangle, at the core of the family nexus. I have indicated the importance of acknowledging the necessary tension within that nexus, and its creative as well as destructive potential. The temptation, or the drive (call it what you will), is always to dissolve the threesome into a less conflictual seeming twosome. In practice, this tendency most often finds expression in the two-parent family becoming the one-parent family. One is liable in this connection to think here mainly of the single mother as the parent remaining in charge, rather than the single father, since it is the latter who often ends up absent, either wilfully or by being discarded. Equally important, although sometimes better disguised, is the obliteration of the mother at another level, not necessarily through her physical absence from the family, but through society's failure (and that of government's, in particular) to recognize the importance of her contribution to the nurturing of her child and thereby her inestimable contribution to the promotion of a healthy and mature society generally. Winnicott (1986, p. 125) put down this blocking out of recognition of the maternal contribution to the universal "fear of WOMAN" (he always used capitals in this context). Bound up with this disparagement was an unavowed fear, especially in the male, of the dependency experienced as an infant. (The girl, after all, knows that in time she will be able to create her own babies.) Winnicott saw evidence of this fear at work in society, particularly in the tendency of men to dominate in the political and economic spheres, and in the easy tolerance of submission towards an overweening leader. (I incline to think that he might have regarded the current insistence of party leaders to be "charismatic" as symptomatic of this.)

Transposing these observations to the evolving picture of care provision from 1948 to the present, one can perhaps discern signs of a move, from a two-parent to a single-parent provider model. One can see this in the progressive shift towards centralization, managerialization, audit, and control of services from the top-down, along with the corresponding downgrading of care as nurturing in favour of care as safeguarding. Whereas the two-parent provider model prescribes a practitioner and an enabler of that provision through the requisite structure, the single-parent provider model prescribes an omni-provider and a group of subordinates, functionaries, at different levels, tasked with carrying through the requisite provision. It can seem almost as if social workers were childminders, acting on behalf of a parent state, and a single parent state at that.

The prevalence and acceptance of this state of affairs is why, in the book I referred to earlier, I characterized the governmental attitude towards its responsibilities as having shifted from a generalized duty to care in 1948, equivalent of what now passes for a statutory "duty *of* care", towards a present-day "duty *to* care" directly for those in need. Implied here, too, is the suggestion that the move from a two-parent to a one-parent model has come about not so much by necessity as by governmental choice, even if that choice was never clearly articulated or posed as an option to the electorate. What I am suggesting is that a range of political and social options have contributed to a situation arising in which it is now ingrained in popular consciousness that government nationally determines and dictates large areas of moral and social education, social provision, and social monitoring— areas that once were the unquestioned province of the family and the local community. Where are concerns about children's obesity, television watching, access to internet sites, attitudes to bullying and racism, information and instruction in sex education, given expression and addressed? The answer: they are expressed in government documents and the primary forum in which they are addressed is in the schoolroom.

There may be complaints aplenty about the reach of the "nanny state", but there nevertheless seems to be widespread compliance with government taking charge in these areas. It seems to be taken as axiomatic that government has a duty to care as a quasi-parent, and that it is ultimately accountable if the nation's children grow up overweight, antisocial, and unprepared for parenthood or citizenship.

If this is the case, can anything be done to redress the situation? This paper has attempted to analyse rather than prescribe, and I do not intend to change this focus at its conclusion by offering a series of simple and inevitably simplistic solutions. All I would say in terms of a recommendation (not a remedy) is that there is a case for government undertaking a thorough-going review, one conducted outside the purely political sphere, about what should pertain to family, to community, and to government in the matter of the social upbringing of children. Perhaps this could take the form of a Royal Commission, but one in which the opinions of ordinary parents and their children, as well as the opinions of those cared for under the aegis of children's departments, past as well as present, are taken into account. What does being a mature member of society mean in our present age? Is Winnicott's dual emphasis on the importance of mental and emotional independence for true maturity on the one hand, and on the risks of fostering compliance as a primary aim of social education in bringing about conditions for a totalitarian state under an individual or collective dictatorship on the other, any longer relevant or sustainable in an era of instant information and exposure to mass communication? These are some of the questions that could usefully be addressed.

My analysis has suggested that the present structure of social provision in which so much to do with the parenting function is centrally determined and controlled, is not only unsatisfactory but ultimately unviable. The State may have taken on a parental role of sorts, but it cannot function properly in the guise of an omni-competent single parent. Moreover, if it cannot ever allow itself to fail (even though it must), and cannot acknowledge its own failings, it can never succeed in being a "good-enough parent" either.

References

Children Act 1948, Geo. V1. London: H.M.S.O.

Children Act 1975, Eliz, II. London H.M.S.O.

Cretney, S. M. (1998). *Law, Law Reform and the Family*. Oxford: Clarendon Press.

Davis, M. & Wallbridge, D. (1981). *Boundary and Space: An Introduction to the Work of D. W. Winnicott*. London: Karnac.

Heywood, J. (1978). *Children in Care: The Development of the Service for the Deprived Child* (revised edn). London: Routledge & Kegan Paul.

Isaacs, S. (Ed.) (1941). *The Cambridge Evacuation Survey.* London: Methuen & Co.

Parton, N. (2004). From Maria Colwell to Victoria Climbié: Reflections on public inquiries into child abuse a generation apart. *Child Abuse Review, 13(2):* 80–94.

Poor Law Act 1930, Geo. V. London H.M.S.O.

Reeves, C. (2006a). A duty to care: Reflections on the influence of Bowlby and Winnicott on the 1948 Children Act. In: J. Issroff (Ed.), *Donald Winnicott and John Bowlby: Personal and Professional Perspectives* (pp. 179–207). London: Karnac.

Reeves, C. (2006b). Singing the same tune? Bowlby and Winnicott on deprivation and delinquency. In: J. Issroff (Ed.), *Donald Winnicott and John Bowlby: Personal and Professional Perspectives* (pp. 71–100). London: Karnac.

Report of the Local Authority and Allied Personal Social Services 1968. Command Paper 3703. London: H.M.S.O.

Summary of the Main Provisions of the Children Bill 1948. Command Paper 7306. London: H.M.S.O.

Winnicott, D. W. (1960). The family and emotional maturity. In: *The Family and Individual Development* (pp. 88–94). London: Tavistock Publications, 1965.

Winnicott, D. W. (1962). Ego integration in child development. In: *The Maturational Processes and the Facilitating Environment* (pp. 56–63). London: Hogarth Press, 1965.

Winnicott, D. W. (1964). *The Child, the Family and the Outside World.* London: Penguin.

Winnicott, D. W. (1968). Adolescent immaturity. In: C. Winnicott, R. Shepherd & M. Davis (Eds.), *Home is Where We Start From* (pp. 150–166). London: Penguin.

Winnicott, D. W. (1986). The price of disregarding psychoanalytical research. In: C. Winnicott, R. Shepherd & M. Davis (Eds.), *Home is Where We Start From.* London: Penguin.

Winnicott, D. W. & Britton, C. (1947). Residential management as a treatment for difficult children. In: C. Winnicott, R. Shepherd, & M. Davis (Eds.), *Deprivation and Delinquency* (pp. 54–72). London: Tavistock Publications.

Winnicott's delinquent

Ann Horne

"The Antisocial Tendency", a paper given before the British Psychoanalytic Society in 1956, is neither Winnicott's first nor last word on the subject of delinquency and antisocial behaviour. It could, however, be said to be the Winnicottian "word" most remembered by his readers on the subject. You may recall the child whom he describes in that talk: his first child analytic training patient. Winnicott had thus not only trained in medicine and specialized in paediatrics but had completed his psychoanalytic training and was commencing the further two years of supervised child and adolescent work necessary to become a child analyst at the Institute of Psychoanalysis. One can understand why trainees find this paper both helpful and extremely reassuring: Winnicott describes how the boy broke into his locked car, jump-started it in the driveway of the clinic, bumped it down to the bottom, flooded the clinic basement and, as Winnicott confesses here and in a later paper, bit Winnicott on the buttocks—three times. As a trainee, I often thought, "But why doesn't he sit down?" That is, when I wasn't thinking, "Well, if Winnicott can describe so honestly his struggles with an acting-out lad, the tussles that I am having may just be worth it!" It was many years later before I began to wonder about the clinic—the Institute of Psychoanalysis itself—that had forbidden Winnicott's continuing with this disruptive lad, whether it had been drawn into a response to delinquency that we find all too often in societal reactions today.

Context

Let us look at the context in which Winnicott was writing in 1956. The study of criminology had become established late in the previous century, perhaps a due progression from the humanitarian interests of penal reformers, and engaging enquiring minds from law, medicine, philosophy, anthropology, and the nascent discipline of sociology. Early themes included the urgent need for a fair system of justice that applied to all and for a range of penalties and punishment that might "fit the crime". *Plus ça change* ... Cesare Lombroso's (1876) experiments in measuring the facial physiognomy of the adult criminal were not untypical of the Italian anthropological school and, in the next century, were to be followed by examination of the body shape of the population—the famous endomorph, ectomorph, and mesomorph of Sheldon (1940, 1942), who rather naively attempted to link character to somatotype, especially criminal character traits in men. Such pursuits of the physical and biological were, in their origin, part of the surge of scientific experiment of the mid- to late nineteenth century and it is striking that character and personality were being examined in this way. During the same period, Henry Maudsley was exploring the boundary between criminality and insanity. Although this was often polemically stated in his writings, he did reach a sense of what he called "individual or family degeneration", which had crime as one of its manifestations, that is, there was an early recognition of environmental factors. Equally, he wrote, "[n]ow it is only a question of degree and kind of fault how far antisocial feeling, thought and conduct, passing through their divers forms of degeneracy, must go before it becomes madness or crime", and "crime is a sort of outlet in which their unsound tendencies are discharged; they would go mad if they were not criminals, and they do not go mad because they are criminals" (Maudsley, 1867, p. 105). The language may not be what we might use now; however, the theoretical propositions stay of interest and the idea of activity, delinquency, and abusing as a defence against psychosis or breakdown remains an important one in psychoanalysis today.

Freud's arrival on the scene was to engage thinking on crime for several decades as psychoanalysis, the new "scientific thinking", brought its own understanding of the "criminal character". Freud wrote one major paper on the subject of criminality—"Criminals (or 'criminality') from a sense of guilt" (Freud, 1925). The emphasis on the unconscious seeking of punishment as a consequence of unresolved Oedipal longings was central. Thus the focus was on the super-ego, the conscience, and its development being impelled by the Oedipal resolution and the move into latency. This remained the key part of psychoanalytic understanding of the antisocial tendency for the next few decades.

In the same year, Freud wrote the foreword to August Aichhorn's *Wayward Youth*. Aichhorn is one of the very few people to whom Winnicott actually refers—his own self-confessed "delinquency" perhaps evident in his refusal to acknowledge the thinking of others in his sources, preferring to state, as he does in "Primitive emotional development" that:

> I shall not first give a historical survey and show the development of my ideas from the theories of others, because my mind doesn't work that way. What happens is I gather this and that, here and there, settle down to clinical experience, form my own theories, and then, last of all, interest myself to see where I stole what. Perhaps this is as good a way as any.

> (Winnicott, 1945, p. 145)

In *Wayward Youth*, Aichhorn follows Freud as to superego development but most interestingly outlines what he terms two "faulty developments" in the child's mental structure (Aichhorn, 1925, pp. 199–224):

• There has been no move from the pleasure principle to the reality principle (one might think here of the Kleinian depressive position or Winnicott's process of disillusionment). The consequence is that the child remains—and has to do so—ego-centric and omnipotent in his functioning, there being no process in conjunction with the environment that allows him to be gently let down from this at a pace with which he can cope. This, Aichhorn writes, has resulted from either too indulgent or too severe treatment. In this we may be forgiven if we hear the voice of Winnicott and the later genesis of the concept of the good-enough mother. Emphatically, Aichhorn recognized the importance of environment: one can see how he engages with this in his talks to lay people, especially where he explicates the technique of child guidance and work with parents (see Aichhorn, 1964—a posthumous collection).

- Aichhorn's second major point is one that, I think, we need to attend to today. In stating that there has been a malformation of the ego ideal and hence the superego, he is locating the insult to the developing child at an earlier stage than Freud, although he keeps faith with the master in asserting that this failure or misdirection of the ego ideal impacts on superego development. The ego ideal is one of these really useful psychoanalytic concepts. It is that sense you can see in the growing toddler of "Who am I? Who do I want to be?" and critically "How do I want the world to view me?" Thus we internalize the expectations and attributes of key objects—adults—in our lives and develop a sense of person, of the self, whom we are satisfied to be. The role of available adults for identification matters here, and the role of shame is crucial—the sense of shame appears when one feels that one has fallen short of this ego ideal. This is important when we have in mind the current concern about adolescents, knife crime, and the role of fathers. For the past few years headlines have asserted "No role models, breakdown of discipline and a culture of violence"—that particular article being written by a black youth worker in London, a research fellow at the Centre for Policy Studies (Bailey, 2007).

In comparing two groups of asocial children, Aichhorn found one to have developed ego ideals but in identification with antisocial parents, hence inevitably coming into conflict not with family but with society. The other group had life experiences characterized by lack of attachments and meaningful identifications; the ego ideal either did not develop or was weak, with the consequence that it could not be a force for achievement or self-regulation in life.

It is also worth noting Aichhorn's comments about those who work with "wayward" young people. At first—and remember that he was a teacher by trade, running a residential establishment for delinquent youth on the outskirts of Vienna, before he trained as a psychoanalyst—he affirms that the work requires people of firm moral stance, able to sustain this in the face of considerable challenge. Later—as evidenced in his letters, noted by Young-Bruehl (1989, pp. 301–302) in her biography of Anna Freud—he comments that the therapist who works best with such young people should be in touch with his own delinquency. Perhaps Winnicott's delinquency, then, is a useful attribute?

Finally in these first years, Melanie Klein wrote in 1927 of "Criminal tendencies in normal children". Although she followed Freud in centring on the development of the superego, the growth of the conscience, she proposed that the superego in delinquency worked in a different direction, rejecting "the desires belonging to the oedipus complex" (Klein, 1927, p. 184). Today, we may consider that there can be two superegos at work, one antisocial, directed to the external world, externalized onto society, and the other internal, conflicted, more depressive, linked to the ego ideal.

The interest of psychoanalysts in delinquency grew. Analysts, in particular Edward Glover, were prominent in the formation of the Institute for the Scientific Treatment of Delinquency—later the Institute for the Study and Treatment of Delinquency (ISTD)—in 1932 and its clinical wing, the Portman Clinic, in 1933. In the archives, we find record cards indicating that Bowlby spent time working with clinic patients, as did Bion. Glover, of course, was director, and another analyst, Kate Friedlander, an involved colleague. The main writings bow to Freud in emphasizing superego formation and Oedipal resolution (Friedlander, 1947; Glover, 1949). However, Glover interestingly proposed that not all antisocial young people needed psychoanalysis and in 1950 made clear his distinction between *functional stress* (which we might connect to the normal developmental processes of puberty and adolescence and which he termed "transitory") and defensive symptomatic reactions to Oedipal conflict where therapy is indicated (Glover, 1950, p. 110).

In the period just before the 1939–1945 war, Bowlby was engaged on the early stages of what became his life work on attachment. His study *Forty-four Juvenile Thieves*, unsurprisingly to us today, places maternal deprivation and separation at the centre of risk factors in the development of an antisocial stance (Bowlby, 1944). His "affectionless children", a category descriptive of the bulk of persistent offenders in his survey, suffer from deficit rather than conflict, an absence of mothering in the first six months (Bowlby, 1944, p. 113).

Finally, mention should be made of the festschrift for Aichhorn, edited by Eissler in 1949. I would like to allude to only two of the many contributors to this but both important when thinking of the antisocial child. Anna Freud's (1949) paper "Certain types and stages of social maladjustment" is a classic. She emphasizes "early disturbance of object-love" consequent on absent, neglectful, ambivalent, or unstable mothering, or multiple impersonal carers, meaning the child cannot invest emotionally in parent figures, so retreats to the self, the body and its needs, which "retain a greater importance than normal" (Freud, 1949, p. 194). This absence of "good-enough mothering" is also problematic in relation to aggression, agency, and potency, which are not met with understanding and containment, and may manifest themselves on a spectrum ranging from "overemphasized aggressivesness" to "wanton destructiveness". Thus the onset, or otherwise, of what is perceived as, or becomes, antisocial behaviour, depends on whether or not there is sufficient maternal attunement and whether or not there is a carer present who can understand the child's gesture, offer containment, and modulate the response.

Jeanne Lampl-De Groot is not frequently quoted when delinquency is discussed, yet her paper "Neurotics, delinquents and ideal formation" is, I think, essential reading (Lampl-de Groot, 1949). She returns us to Aichhorn's preoccupation with the ego ideal, concluding that the prerequisites are a capacity for identification and objects (key adults or siblings) with whom to identify. Again, with recent news stories in mind, we are directed to the issue of role models and the availability of identifications. Her comments on the capacity of a strong ego and ego ideal to make use of aggression and gain a sense of agency reminds us of Winnicott's writing on muscularity and the need of the infant for a mother who meets and survives the ruthlessness of the infant (Winnicott, 1963c).

Winnicott and the antisocial child

Such was the theoretical world when Winnicott wrote about his first training case. Although, as I stated at the start of this chapter, the major paper one remembers is "The Antisocial Tendency", it is worth recalling that Winnicott also wrote about delinquency prior to 1956. He was one of that important triumvirate of John Bowlby, Emanuel Miller, and Donald Winnicott who famously wrote to the *British Medical Journal* in December 1939, concerned about the proposals for the evacuation of children from London in the face of the outbreak of World War II. Quoting Bowlby's work, they stress that it "showed that one important external factor in the causation of persistent delinquency is a small child's separation from his mother", concluding: "If these opinions are correct it follows that evacuation of small children without their mothers can lead to very serious and widespread psychological disorder. For instance, it can lead to a big increase in juvenile delinquency in the next decade" (Bowlby, Miller & Winnicott, 1939, pp. 13–14).

Indeed, the wartime Beveridge Report led to the establishment in 1948 of the Welfare State which tackled issues of health, deprivation, education, poverty, and housing. Onlookers were appalled to note that the rate of juvenile delinquency did not decrease subsequently but grew. This is not a perverse accusation that evacuees caused this wave of anti-social behaviour; rather, it indicates that we should also be thinking of the absence and loss of *fathers* consequent on war—and the absence of role models.

Prior to this, Winnicott had read to the British Psychoanalytic Society a paper on "The manic defence" in which he gave two asocial children as examples. The terms used were heavily based on the formulations of Melanie Klein and the emphasis here, in 1935, was on strengthening "good internal objects", internalizing a good object to countermand the anxieties that lead to activity as a defence. Again, we are in the arena of what key adults are available to the child, how the sense of self can develop and be strengthened by the internalization of good experiences; and again we might think of present concerns about violent youth. Finally, in a paper dated simply "1940s" we find him pondering: "I cannot get away from my clinical experience of the relation of not being wanted at the start of life to the subsequent antisocial tendency" (Winnicott, 1940, pp. 52–53).

This seems to be a matter of primary privation and is in contrast to his thoughts in "The Antisocial Tendency".

In "The Antisocial Tendency" Winnicott's young training patient is sent to Approved School. It is often thought that Winnicott is here proposing that psychoanalysis is not a treatment of choice for delinquency—indeed, he distinguished between the antisocial tendency (which is also part of development) and the more formed delinquent structure. However:

> It can easily be seen that treatment for this boy should have been not psychoanalysis but placement. Psychoanalysis only made sense

if added after placement. Since this time I have watched analysts of all kinds fail in the psychoanalysis of antisocial children.

By contrast the following story brings out the fact that an antisocial tendency may sometimes be treated very easily if the treatment be adjunctive to specialised environmental care.

(Winnicott, 1956, p. 307)

One might expect the story that follows to describe residential care; in fact, the boy, who suffers a compulsion to steal in it, is "treated" by his mother's interventions, guided by Winnicott's advice. "Specialized environmental care" can mean family. We might like to reflect on the intensity of intervention necessary, what is good enough to get a child back on a developmental track and what is supportive of this.

Winnicott emphasizes that the antisocial tendency both stems from deprivation and contains a sense of hope. He is therefore describing a very different child from Bowlby's "affectionless child" who has never had an experience of something good, who has suffered an absence of early emotional attunement. The Winnicottian child seeks that which he once had, making a demand and claim on the environment for what is his right, for what he once had that has been lost.

The paper continues to develop the dual axis of stealing (plus lying) and destructiveness, the former clearly linked to object-seeking. The "nuisance value" is a vital part—that the environment is made to pay attention. The "cure" for Winnicott lies in the finding of object love, the capacity to engage with an attuned adult, and the capacity to feel despair as well as hope, to mourn. He alters his stance on psychoanalysis as the paper develops, insisting by the end that management (e.g., in residential care) is the intervention of choice and not therapy, while still commenting in the final sentence on what the analyst must expect both in and out of the therapy room. Having it both ways is not uncommon in Winnicott!

For an analyst wedded to the concept of five-times-a-week analysis, this was quite a step backwards—or forwards. For present-day practitioners, more accustomed to the benefits of once or twice weekly work and to engaging robustly and creatively with networks around a child, it feels a little false to be polarizing either analysis or management. How one copes with *both* is our issue today.

I would posit that Winnicott's delinquent with a sense of hope is less commonly found in our clinics today; rather the child traumatized early, often at a stage before speech can begin to make sense of life, and suffering primary privation, who causes concern through his activity-based defences, is more likely to be referred. However, I make a brief diversion.

A note on the interesting times that followed

At the time Winnicott wrote "The Antisocial Tendency" (1956), criminology had begun its move away from psychoanalytic theories of criminal behaviour. Durkheim's work of the previous century on anomie, exclusion, the division of labour, and the normality of crime had been translated into English (Durkheim, 1893, 1895) and social critique became the growing focus; Terence Morris was about to publish his work on criminal families and, particularly, the criminal area; later researchers would focus on poverty and social deprivation. In the Child Guidance Clinics, the influence of a more systemic family approach to understanding and helping struggling children was beginning to be felt. The development of family therapy, albeit arising from the work of psychoanalytically informed practitioners, in many places struck a considerable blow against psychoanalysis and its particular understanding.

One could make three points here:

- The concept of the criminal family and criminal area is not in contradiction to psychoanalytic theory; rather, it supports those who would see the development of the ego ideal as crucial in the child's taking up an antisocial position as the only possible one. Identification is with criminal relatives and peers—an issue that has been sadly in the news recently in relation to the use of knives amongst young adolescents and their identifications with violent role models. I shall return to the sense of shame and humiliation that is part of the ego ideal constellation and is such a part of the psychological structure of violent young people.
- There was in the 1960s the start of an unhelpful polarizing of therapies available to those who worked with distressed children and adolescents. It is perhaps a part of the establishment of any new theoretical approach that its proselytizers denigrate others, idealize their own approach, and institutionalize the results. This certainly

happened to psychoanalysis as an intervention and it did *not* rise with any potency to the challenge. Perhaps now we are better at holding together the value in a range of approaches, and we certainly need this in relation to the complex cases we see today. At the time, it felt as if the baby was being thrown out with the bath water, that the value of a psychoanalytic understanding was lost in the debate as to who pursued the better therapeutic method. The same happened in criminological theory as it seemingly set off on a course in search of the equivalent of the philosopher's stone, the one true theory of crime. Life is more complex, as criminologists now realize. Indeed, such a tendency to polarize into "either—or", one might point out, is in itself typical of adolescent processes, typical of the dilemmas in which adolescents find themselves and of the imperatives they project onto adults.

• Third, this movement frequently involved quite a gross misrepresentation of psychoanalytic thinking by its critics, presenting psychoanalysis as an approach that blamed the individual and, in offering "treatment", focused on individual "illness" and not on societal responsibility. The medical model—"illness" rather than psychological processes—became an issue. Again, there was a tendency to polarize—*either* a focus on individual psychopathology *or* on family, social policy, and environment. It seemed impossible to hold both together, to understand that recognizing processes at work in the individual did not mean ignoring or denying the importance of the environment.

The theoretical toolkit today

In an excellent chapter in Judith Issroff's book on Winnicott and Bowlby, Christopher Reeves finds Winnicott's "delinquent with a sense of hope" an insufficient concept when one is faced with young people in trouble today (Reeves, 2006, p. 96). I agree with this. It is rare to encounter the Winnicottian delinquent today—more common to find the privation that he noted in his earlier writing. Reeves helpfully directs his readers to the work of Barbara Dockar-Drysdale (1968, 1973, 1990) (greatly influenced in her work in residential therapeutic care by her relationship with Winnicott) and her concept of the "frozen child" (Dockar-Drysdale, 1990, p. 180), akin to Bowlby's affectionless child. She writes:

These need to reach depression (usually very deep). This is the most delinquent group. The depression is followed by dependence on one person. In communication with this person he will need to learn the nature of delinquency and its cause, his severe early deprivation. He will also need to learn that delinquency is a form of addiction, which could be described as self-provision accompanied by intense excitement; it is to this excitement that the boy becomes addicted, and the depression which he reaches through dependence has much in common with withdrawal symptoms.

(Dockar-Drysdale, 1990, pp. 180–181)

Clinical experience would agree with this, as with her formulation of "archipelago children" (Dockar-Drysdale, 1990, p. 179) who have what I have called "atoll-like egos", requiring long-term developmental therapy on the lines that Anne Hurry has described in the Anna Freud Centre (Hurry, 1998). Feeling states are overwhelming to the child with the immature sense of self and must be externalized. Work thus often involves slowly naming such states, leading to the capacity to recognize, anticipate, and tolerate them.

The addiction described by Dockar-Drysdale can be found in the activity-seeking delinquent who often seeks experiences of fearfulness and high anxiety. The case I will describe later illustrates such processes. This activity involves replay of the body experiences emanating from early trauma—just as adolescents who self-harm by cutting can become addicted to the release of the body's natural morphine when they do this, so the young person whose defences are centred on the body and activity can repeat sensations of fear and adrenaline rush. The latter can become physically compelling; the former leads to a repetition of the fear in the hope of this time gaining mastery. It is a repetition-compulsion.

It is apparent that, following Winnicott, the work of Khan (1963) on cumulative trauma has to be a further part of our intellectual toolkit. Pre-verbal trauma, especially through an experience of severe physical and/or sexual abuse, would appear to be a feature of those young people referred to us today. In the absence of any attentive object—and the presence of corrupt objects—the child has only recourse to the primary body-ego, which remains a solution and recourse when anxiety later appears. As Khan reminds us, later traumata may appear minor but to the child traumatized early, there has been no development of a protective function that reduces the impact of these. Again, developmental psychotherapy is necessary.

Briefly, one also has the work of Glasser (1996) on the core complex, the problems of the vicious circle—the search for an idealized intimacy, a growing sense of engulfment, and the need for violence in order to regain a sense of integrity of the self. The consequent feelings of isolation and abandonment result in a resumption of the search for the perfect close relationship. His concept of self-preservative violence is also important, especially in relation to those young offenders who seem to explode unpredictably into violence (Glasser, 1998).

I'd like to say a few further words about the ego ideal and the sense of shame. Don Campbell's concept of "the shame shield" as a protective function, one that he found to have been constantly breached in the sexually abusing adolescents of whom he wrote (Campbell, 1994), is helpful. The development of the ego ideal is bound up with the sense of shame which emerges when we feel we have fallen short of our ideal. Shame takes us out of the limelight—we cover our faces, retreat—and it gives us space to recover from the humiliation. Children treated with violence and abuse have often been exposed to constant and recurring humiliation—the shame shield ceases to function and, as in Khan's cumulative trauma, small slights can then be experienced as massive insults, calling up the memory of the trauma. The obverse of shame is perhaps respect. In this, two things come to mind:

- the recent Labour government's "respect agenda" for young people which seemed to focus on the respect due by the adolescent to adults and society rather than that due to the young person; and
- the importance of humiliation in the genesis of violence. This is as true of delinquent violence as it is of terrorism. The phrase "He dissed me"—that is, he disrespected me—is an important one in youth culture.

Finally, when we think developmentally we also have to think of the normality of an antisocial stance in adolescence. It is, after all, part of separation and individuation and we must learn—like Glover—to take a light but containing approach to those whose delinquency is transient. Most delinquents, after all, grow out of it, mainly by developing relationships in early adulthood. The "ASBO culture" is interesting in relation to this. Developed as an intervention intended to deal with nuisance in society, the Anti-Social Behaviour Order was meant to be a way of coping with antisocial neighbours and other adults; that it has come to be used so frequently with children is of interest and at times concern—particularly as breaching an ASBO takes one from civil to criminal jurisdiction and may result in a criminal conviction. I think it is worth thinking about the possibilities of containment in the ASBO—an environment that can respond and hold steady—and the risks of a criminal record. The current imbalance is worth discussing. Winnicott would have seen the robust containment that he required of the environment; he would also, one feels, have been concerned about the lack of flexibility and the danger of criminalizing the young inherent in the legislation. Several counties have been taken to task by central government for not issuing many ASBOs. Not many of us realized that there was yet another hidden government target here! It is impressive that these councils had actually grasped the problem and increased their Youth Service provision, numbers of youth workers, and facilities for young people—known factors in counteracting delinquent and antisocial activity and in engaging with adolescents. The horror is that this was not recognized—that their creativity had, in Winnicottian terms, moved to meet the creativity of the young—and was punished. We need awareness of the polarization of responses to the child or young person who *acts*—the absence of thought infuses our responses, and our reactions can be as knee-jerk as the adolescent's. This is particularly true of policy: our policymakers remain at high risk of advocating reactive, knee-jerk, and simplistically populist legislation.

One young delinquent—Matthew

I thought it might be helpful to give a flavour of a session with a young antisocial lad. I hope you will be able to see the issues of intimacy and distance, of activity and thought, of excitement and sadness, of seeking to repeat sensations, and the problems inherent in hope. In accordance with Winnicott, we ensured that there was a resilient environment, placement, and support before therapy began.

Matthew was referred at age 14 for sexually interfering with the 6 year-old sister of a friend. This friend often had intercourse with his girlfriend in the presence of other adolescents (both exciting and offensive to Matthew). The abusive incident occurred when all had been watching a particularly humiliating exit from the World Cup by the England football team.

Briefly Matthew's history was of parental warfare and paternal depression: his father being ejected by his mother when Matthew was two years old; an abusive boyfriend (Sean) immediately moving in; his mother's death (query suicide) when he was five; time spent with the stepgrandfather who had sexually abused Matthew's mother when *her* mother died; a long struggle for custody by his father and paternal grandmother as his mother's Will had directed him to stay with Sean. He finally moved to live with his father and stepmother and was immediately in trouble in school aged seven. Finally a good school for children with emotional and behavioural difficulties took him in.

This session occurred early in December, almost nine months into once-weekly therapy. Matthew at this point is fifteen and is living with his grandmother during the week to sustain his schooling as his father and stepmother have moved some distance away. He has a stepsister—daughter of his stepmother—and a half-brother, child of his father's second marriage.

Matthew arrived early for his session, wearing a new, padded, warm jacket. (He had come the previous week in a sweatshirt and with an awful cold.) Although his cold was still bad, he said that he was OK, that he had taken lots of soup. This comment came with a smile—in our last session he had told me that his grandmother was very good at making soup. (Paternal grandmother has transference implications—at one point Matthew briefly wondered if I, too, listened to Capital Gold.) He hadn't been allowed to take a day off school, however. I wondered if he could have been able to bear that—not being active and just sitting with his thoughts. He agreed he could not; he would rather be in school. I reflected inwardly on this unusually intimate start and wondered when reaction would set in. (When Matthew attends, he always takes and needs time to re-discover his object: he seems, indeed, to expect a corrupt object.)

There was a sustained pause. He looked very sad. I wondered if he were thoughtful now or just fed up? Fed up. His father had said that the moped was too much for his Christmas gift and he probably wouldn't get it. He expanded on how it would have cost £200. His father was giving his brother Alex a computer worth £200; Matthew would get a new mobile phone worth £100; and his sister, Emma, a present worth £75. There was a pause, half sad, half angry. I wondered rather weakly if that seemed unfair? *Yes*—Alex gets everything. (Alex, indulged at age five, contrasts with Matthew, abused and abandoned.)

After a further pause Matthew wondered if his father would give him the money and he could put it towards a bike himself. Then he deflated, recalling that his father preferred to pay things up week-by-week. I said that it seemed impossible for the adults to get things right for him. We reflected in silence.

"Do you know a Pa.. Po.. something like that—it's a bike." It emerged as a Piaggio. "They're *very* nice! I really like them. I was out last night on one!" I felt anxiety begin to rise and wondered inside about this need to make the adult anxious, and why. There followed a story of Matthew and five or six friends. Dave had brought the bike and all had tried it out in the local park. Steve did a "wheelie" and drove into a tree. Matthew also tried it—"It was really good!" He described sharp turns, sudden acceleration, mud flying, and excitement. As he was in full flow, his mobile phone rang. He looked apologetic, muttered, "Sorry," said the answering service would pick it up, and could not resist checking the screen. It was Dave leaving a message: "He already phoned twice when I was on the train coming here! It's about meeting tonight." The phone was switched off and put away. He continued with the bike tale—taking it out on the road out of town, a vivid description of Dave nearly coming off the back of the bike as Matthew accelerated—"It can do 45 miles an hour!"—and finally the return to town.

I thought about the sense of life and energy in the midst of this extremely dangerous behaviour. "You know, you really like being 'on the edge', don't you!" Matthew looked questioning. I said that on the bike he liked being in control himself (he didn't like being on the back) but it could tip over—Steve had managed to hit a tree. I suggested he was also "on the edge" with the police, should he be found, and with the court, as the judge had told him that his return to court on any count would mean a custodial sentence. And he had told me before (in an earlier session) that being on a bike could be scary and he didn't like that. "Yes, that's why I won't let Steve drive."

There was a pause. I interpreted then that it was interesting that this "on the edge" excitement had actually followed a very painful description of him and Emma feeling "on the edge" in the family. He gave me a very direct look. I offered that one way he had learned of being in control of these very difficult, sad feelings was through the excited "on the edge" feelings, but they were risky. I wondered, too, about the excitement keeping *me* "on the edge", unsure of his safety, and wondered if he was good at making the adults and me feel this. He smiled gently.

There was quite a long pause. Matthew launched into a story of his friend, Joseph, a very small fourteen year-old. Joseph's passion was cars—with a particular emphasis on taking and driving them away. I noted to myself the connection between my interpretation of the pain in the family and his further recourse to excitement and danger, moving from bikes to cars, but did not interrupt. Matthew gave great detail of how Joseph would break into the black boxes behind the steering wheel panel, where to locate these in a Rover Metro, and diverted into a variety of ways to break into a car. Joseph had been doing this since he was seven years-old. The police knew him well—had been to see him the other day as he is the first port of call when cars go missing. "He has been cautioned and the police know him. Pathetic!" "Pathetic—who?" I asked. "Joe. He knows they'll come to see him first. When he takes a car he drives with the headlights on full beam so that he can't be seen himself. He just gets very excited by cars. Once when I was with him he saw a Jaguar. I said, 'NO!' but Joe kept talking about what it would be like to drive it when we were walking away." I wondered if Joe had the same sense of excitement in relation to cars that Matthew had talked of with bikes. He looked surprised: "No, he's pathetic." I commented that sometimes things are both pathetic and exciting, reminding him of the 36" television set he said his father had bought that in one way seemed pathetic to him but in another seemed full of excitement and potential. This had been in an earlier session. He grinned—"That's true!" I continued, "So you know some things that are both pathetic-daft-dangerous and pathetic-exciting-'on the edge'?" He nodded thoughtfully.

The story of Joe continued. He had "torched" a car. This felt suddenly very unsafe, as if the juxtaposition of "pathetic" and "excitement" had to be avoided. He had tried to break into a car in Tesco's car park (the known area where local youth find and dump cars and bikes) but couldn't get at the black box. Realizing that he had left his fingerprints all over the vehicle, he had found a cloth and jerrycan of petrol in the boot and poured it over the front seats, leaving the can in the car before striking a match. He had singed his hair. "He's totally pathetic! He could have burned himself badly. He had the rag from the boot—he could have wiped off his fingerprints. He ran off and it went

'Whump!' exploding. The Fire Brigade was called. He could have hurt people!" Matthew sounded very upset. I said gently that I thought he had witnessed this, been there with Joe. He nodded. I added that it was frightening that the excitement and "on the edge" bits could tip right over into danger and wondered if he scared himself. He nodded, saying, "He could have been harmed!" Yes. After a pause I added that it was interesting that such a memory of danger had followed my saying to him that he wanted me to feel "on the edge" sometimes—that he was letting me know how dreadfully dangerous things sometimes felt for him and that it was right that we were both concerned.

He recalled a teacher at school, in car mechanics class, whom Matthew had asked something that implied how to hot-wire cars. The teacher had given him the information and not asked why he wanted to know. I said I thought he was letting me know about two things. First, grown-ups may not be straight but may collude with exciting, illegal things, like the teacher giving him the information. (I was thinking of corrupt objects again.) How, then, could he possibly know to trust me and my concern? Second, perhaps he was warning me that he could be tricky—tricking the teacher and perhaps other grown-ups, like me. He gave me a very direct, straight look.

There was a further pause. Matthew said, "The bike engine's still running." The bike, of course, had been stolen and hot-wired. His friends were "second time thieves", having come across it stolen and abandoned. They had by-passed the ignition and could not turn off the engine. They would have to cover the exhaust pipe, cutting off the air supply. (All endings, I thought, are traumatic—even for the bike.) "Someone stole it last night." I must have looked astonished. "Yeah, when we'd gone home Dave had left it at his back gate and phoned to say it had been taken. We found Steve had taken it and had it at his place. It would have been pathetic if a nicked bike had been nicked—I mean we couldn't report it to the police, could we?" I said that I thought that was really interesting: that, when something has gone wrong in the past, the grown-ups will simply not take a young person seriously. Perhaps in some ways this was a little like Matthew—it is impossible for him to hope that the adults will be concerned *now* for his safety when they made such a bad job of it in the past. "You mean Sean," said Matthew, referring to his mother's abusive boyfriend. "Yes, and everything that happened then. Now, as a result of that, you are making me into another of these grown-ups who hears very dangerous things but can't stop you. Sometimes it feels better to do that than for you to hope that it might be different."

The following pause felt more thoughtful. "I'll only go tonight if Steve has a crash helmet for me. I know he's got one. It *is* scary—but exciting scary." ("Crash helmet" has become equated with me, an interesting parallel when one thinks about heads and minds.) I added that that was why he insists on driving, being in control: "It's like not taking the risk that the adults won't protect you again, but it's also the same 'on the edge' excitement of waiting for something to happen that was awful and too much for you when you were little." Matthew nodded slowly.

It was almost time to stop. Matthew checked the clock and put on his jacket. He told me that he *was* careful as sometimes it could get too scary. Moreover, tonight they wouldn't be on the road but in a farmer's field. I said that he was taking on some of the adult bits about protecting himself but still being "on the edge". He was leaving me with something to worry about—perhaps he needed to do that. He gave a quiet smile and "See you next week!" I thought it was a promise to stay alive.

Conclusion

While we may only rarely encounter Winnicott's delinquent with a sense of hope, who seeks justice for the deprivation he unconsciously feels, our work today with young people cannot proceed without his injunction of "placement first". The containment of the antisocial child may be in a family or an institution but needs to be flexible, resilient, and securely holding. We also need to be in constant communication with one another in our roles in the network surrounding such young people, as the temptation is to polarize, to identify with victim *or* offender parts of the child, and so to cease meaningful communication. Integration is key—for child and for network. Having it both ways, I have said, is a common phenomenon in Winnicott's writings. Perhaps if *we* think "and—and" rather than "either—or", we can see that he had a point!

Winnicott, like Bowlby, engaged with policymakers over issues that he found unacceptable. We, too, need to do this. The resignation of Professor Rod Morgan, first chair of the Youth Justice Board, he said, was related to his insistence that he be allowed to be critical of policy when he felt it to be inappropriate or damaging. Lord Ramsbotham, equally, was outspoken about his shock at conditions for Young Offenders—and was not reappointed as Her Majesty's Chief Inspector of Prisons. What a loss of experience and integrity these departures represent! Like Winnicott, we need to find ways to be heard.

References

Aichhorn, A. (1925). *Wayward Youth*. New York: The Viking Press [reprinted 1935].
Aichhorn, A. (1964). *Delinquency and Child Guidance: Selected Papers*. New York: International Universities Press.
Bailey, S. (2007, 21 March). No role models, breakdown of discipline and a culture of violence. *Evening Standard*.
Bowlby, J. (1944). *Forty-four Juvenile Thieves: Their Characters and Home Life*. London: Tindall & Cox [reprinted 1946].
Bowlby, J., Miller, E. & Winnicott, D. W. (1939). Letter: The evacuation of small children. *British Medical Journal* 16 December 1939. [Reprinted in: Winnicott, C., Shepherd, R. & Davis, M. (Eds.) (1984) *Deprivation and Delinquency* (pp. 13–14). London: Tavistock.]
Campbell, D. (1994). Breaching the shame shield: Thoughts on the assessment of adolescent sexual abusers. *Journal of Child Psychotherapy, 20(3)*: 309–326.
Dockar-Drysdale, B. (1968). *Therapy in Child Care*. London: Longman.
Dockar-Drysdale, B. (1973). *Consultation in Child Care*. London: Longman.
Dockar-Drysdale, B. (1990). *The Provision of Primary Experience: Winnicottian Work with Children and Adolescents*. London: Free Association Books.
Durkheim, E. (1893). *De la Division du travail social, Étude sur l'organisation des sociétés supérieures*. Paris: Presses Universitaires de France [reprinted in English as *The Division of Labour in Society*. London: Macmillan, 1933].
Durkheim, E. (1895). *Les règles de la méthode*. Paris: Librarie Felix Alcan [reprinted in English as *Rules of the Sociological Method*. Glencoe: The Free Press, 1938].
Eissler, K. R. (Ed.) (1949). *Searchlights on Delinquency*. New York: International Universities Press.
Freud, A. (1949). Certain types and stages of social maladjustment. In: K. R. Eissler (Ed.), *Searchlights on Delinquency* (pp. 193–204). New York: International Universities Press.
Freud, S. (1925). Criminals from a sense of guilt. In: *Some Characters Met with in Psychoanalytic Work. S.E., 14* (pp. 332–333). London: Hogarth Press, 1981.
Friedlander, K. (1947). *The Psycho-analytic Approach to Juvenile Delinquency—Theory: Case-Studies: Treatment*. New York: International Universities Press.

Glasser, M. (1996). Aggression and sadism in the perversions. In: I. Rosen (Ed.), *Sexual Deviation* (3rd edn) (pp. 279–299). Oxford: Oxford University Press.

Glasser, M. (1998). On violence: A preliminary communication. *International Journal of Psychoanalysis, 79(5)*: 887–902.

Glover, E. (1949). Outline of the investigation and treatment of delinquency in Great Britain: 1912–1948. In: K. R. Eissler (Ed.), *Searchlights on Delinquency* (pp. 433–452). New York: International Universities Press.

Glover, E. (1950). On the desirability of isolating a "functional" (psychosomatic) group of delinquent disorders. *British Journal of Delinquency, 1*: 104–112.

Hurry, A. (1998). *Psychoanalysis and Developmental Therapy*. London: Karnac.

Khan, M. M. R. (1963). The concept of cumulative trauma. In: *The Privacy of the Self* (pp. 42–58). New York: International Universities Press, 1974.

Klein, M. (1927). Criminal tendencies in normal children. In: *Love, Guilt and Reparation and Other Works* (pp. 170–185). London: Hogarth.

Lampl-De Groot, J. (1949). Neurotics, delinquents and ideal formation. In: K. R. Eissler (Ed.), *Searchlights on Delinquency* (pp. 246–255). New York: International Universities Press.

Lombroso, C. (1876). *L'Uomo delinquente* [*The Criminal Man*]. Milan: Horpli.

Maudsley, H. (1867). *The Pathology of Mind*. London: Macmillan & Co.

Morris, T. (1957). *The Criminal Area: A Study in Social Ecology*. London: Greenwood Press.

Reeves, C. (2006). Singing the same tune? Bowlby and Winnicott on deprivation and delinquency. In: J. Issroff (Ed.), *Donald Winnicott and John Bowlby: Personal and Professional Perspectives* (pp. 71–100). London: Karnac.

Sandler, J., Holder, A. & Meers, D. (1963). The ego ideal and the ideal self. *The Psychoanalytic Study of the Child, 18*: 139–158.

Sheldon, W. (1940). *The Varieties of Human Physique: An Introduction to Constitutional Psychology*. New York: Harper.

Sheldon, W. (1942). *The Varieties of Temperament: A Psychology of Constitutional Differences*. New York: Harper.

Winnicott, D. W. (1935). The manic defence. In: *Through Paediatrics to Psychoanalysis* (pp. 129–144). London: Hogarth Press, 1975.

Winnicott, D. W. (1940). The delinquent and habitual offender. In: R. Shepherd, J. Johns & H. T. Robinson (Eds.), *Thinking about Children* (pp. 51–53). London: Karnac, 1996.

Winnicott, D. W. (1945). Primitive emotional development. In: *Through Paediatrics to Psychoanalysis* (pp. 145–156). London: Hogarth Press, 1975.

Winnicott, D. W. (1950–1955). Aggression in relation to emotional development. In: *Through Paediatrics to Psychoanalysis* (pp. 204–218). London: Hogarth Press, 1975.

Winnicott, D. W. (1956). The Antisocial Tendency. In: *Through Paediatrics to Psychoanalysis* (pp. 306–315). London: Hogarth Press, 1958.

Winnicott, D. W. (1958). Psychoanalysis and the sense of guilt. In: *The Maturational Processes and the Facilitating Environment* (pp. 15–28). London: Hogarth Press, 1979.

Winnicott, D. W. (1959–1964). Classification: Is there a psychoanalytic contribution to psychiatric classification? In: *The Maturational Processes and the Facilitating Environment* (pp. 124–139). London: Hogarth Press, 1979.

Winnicott, D. W. (1960). Counter-transference. In: *The Maturational Processes and the Facilitating Environment* (pp. 158–165). London: Hogarth Press, 1979.

Winnicott, D. W. (1963a). The mentally ill in your caseload. In: *The Maturational Processes and the Facilitating Environment* (pp. 217–229). London: Hogarth Press, 1979.

Winnicott, D. W. (1963b). Psychotherapy of character disorders. In: *The Maturational Processes and the Facilitating Environment* (pp. 203–216). London: Hogarth Press, 1979.

Winnicott, D. W. (1963c). The development of the capacity for concern. In: *The Maturational Processes and the Facilitating Environment* (pp. 73–82). London: Hogarth Press, 1979.

Winnicott, D. W. & Britton, C. (1947). Residential management as a treatment for difficult children. In: C. Winnicott, R. Shepherd & M. Davis (Eds.), *Deprivation and Delinquency* (pp. 54–72). London: Tavistock Publications.

Young-Bruehl, E. (1989). *Anna Freud—A Biography*. London: Macmillan.

Heroic delinquency and the riddle of the Sphinx

Jenny Sprince

Judith Trowell

Introduction

In his paper "The Antisocial Tendency" (1956) Winnicott states that "the antisocial tendency implies hope". He is suggesting that antisocial behaviour calls attention to an unmet need. When it is not met, the individual can go on to become a delinquent.

Winnicott believed that the best treatment for such individuals was not individual psychoanalysis but something he calls "management" (p. 308). He goes on to talk about it being a sign of hope: the young person is looking for something or someone to help; and is needing the environment to be stable enough to cope with his or her behaviour.

I have been reflecting for a long time on delinquency: it is an area of huge public concern as well as one that presents problems for those of us who work psychoanalytically. I am passionately interested in the internal world of children and young people and how we can encourage change when they are in trouble, through interventions that keep in mind both the internal and the external world.

I am currently chair of an organization called VOICE. We work with the two thousand young people currently in prison, the two hundred or so in secure units, and the young people sectioned in mental hospitals. Many of these young people in prison, secure units, or a mental hospital have been violent to themselves or others. This area of work seems to be growing.

I recently went to the young persons' ward at a psychiatric hospital to see a young man who had attacked others for gain. This is a letter he wrote to a senior politician:

Dear Mr XXXX,

I'm writing to say you are nothing but fucking scum and I can't stand you, you fucking cunt and I'm going to fucking kill you and your family as well so if I was you I'd watch your back and you can tell the police cause I don't give a fuck or phone the police.

Fucking scum
YYYYYY

Over the years I have seen a number of boys who stay vividly in my memory. In each case, I wondered why they had taken the path that they did. As a psychiatrist of course I can attach to them some sort of mental health label, but that is usually an arbitrary process that leaves me unsure of how or why they developed as they did, and more importantly what to do next.

The case that stays most vivid in my mind is a family with four children referred for assessment with a single mother: each child had a different father, and as each child arrived they shared mother's bed, alongside her male or female partners (who were various). When the next baby came, the older child moved into his or her own bed in the other room. They were referred because of neglect (gross) and possible sexual abuse. The eldest was a boy of eleven years, then came a girl of nine years, a boy of eight years and the youngest, a girl of five. The eldest did an amazing drawing: an underwater scene with sharks and electric eels and other dangerous creatures, and a tiny male figure trapped in the tentacles of an octopus; the boy agreed with my comment that he felt trapped in the situation he was in. All four children were taken into care and placed in Kent. After a while they were returned home and the eldest boy started to get into trouble. When I saw him he said: "You should not have done it, Dr Trowell. We had a different life and environment and it is impossible to settle at home now we have seen what others have, how they live." Now they were back in their impoverished flat in a very deprived neighbourhood. But whilst they were in care, social services had traced the children's fathers. The eldest boy had an American father who had disappeared. The next girl and the second boy had fathers around, whom they began to see. The second boy had a father in prison. This man encouraged his son—who was very bright—to work hard, and in response the boy demanded his education. He obtained a scholarship to a boarding school. When I last heard of them, the older boy was in prison in Leeds for a string of offences; he was nineteen years-old at the time. The younger boy was doing school exams and flourishing.

The other family I recall in glorious technicolour had nine children by the end. They too were referred for assessment following neglect and possible physical and sexual abuse. The mother, who had a limited IQ, had been abandoned by her husband because she could not care for their three children and he could not stand the situation any longer. One day, when she was out with the three children and the buggy, she met a man at the bus stop: he went home with her and stayed. We learnt later that he had been released from prison just that day after fifteen years, and that he had himself experienced years of sexual abuse. He was a violent man, and controlled and dominated the household. He sexually abused the older three children, and some of his own children as they arrived. He made videos of them and had his friends round to abuse the children—obtaining quite a good income from this. They were all taken into care and we saw them regularly in their respective foster homes, and then subsequently as they drifted back to central London.

The eldest girl was in a flat working the streets. The boy tried to conform, but soon became involved in delinquency and was known to the police. The youngest girl was using drugs and self-harming, so that I had to involve secure accommodation and try to find a place for her. When last seen the boy was on his way to a young offenders' institution. I saw him with his partner and their six month old baby. He was desperate but saw no other life for himself with no qualifications and no way out. His younger sister had a baby that was removed into care. She was living with a very violent young man who had been discharged from the army. They had contacted their father who lived out of London with his new family. He tried to be helpful but felt overwhelmed by the problems involved. Their stepfather and mother each received three months in prison, but then returned to carry on as before. By then, the eldest of their six children was in trouble with the police.

What do I understand from these examples, apart from my own powerlessness to really change things? These young people spent brief periods in care and were then returned home. Their time in care was not long enough, and the placements were not suitable, not sufficiently therapeutic, although the carers were impressive and tried hard.

In the first case, the intervention of the birth fathers for the younger children was significantly helpful; in the second, the destructiveness of the stepfather and the paralysis of the birth father seemed a crucial factor in preventing any helpful outcome. The children experienced some good placements, but the stays were too brief and subsequent arrangements failed. We worked as best we could as an outpatient service, but their attendance was erratic, although we maintained contact over many years.

So I have been very interested in the role of fathers. Hence the book I published with Alicia Etchegoyen (2001)—*The Importance of Fathers*. I do think fathers and their functioning are crucial for the development of the young person's sense of self, their internal world, internal objects, and the ability to manage anger, delay gratification, and work towards a goal and some sense of moral development—never mind Oedipal resolution, recognition of the parental couple, and one's own smallness, one's position in the generations, and the being given up by/separation from mother.

Residential therapeutic communities take on some very troubled and damaged young people, from very similar backgrounds and birth families to the ones I have described above. A residential placement is often seen as a last resort, but for many of these young people a family placement is too intense and cannot be managed. So it may be a last resort, but is also a major therapeutic possibility.

I see a therapeutic residential setting as a place where there are a range of possible relationships on offer, but where at all levels the aim is to contain, to understand, to reflect, and to facilitate emotional growth. Most of the young people placed in such settings have little contact with their external families; the aim is to help them experience benign care from trustworthy adults who can bear their rage, pain, distress, envy, and love. The demands on the adults caring for these young people are intense given the flood of emotions washing around them. It is therefore essential that the staff members are enabled to manage their own feelings and understand and think about them. Otherwise they may respond inappropriately or retaliate to verbal or non-verbal threats by attacking the young person or by becoming caught up in a combative interchange of a sadomasochistic character.

Jenny Sprince

From dysfunctional family to functioning system: the role of therapeutic residential care

In her introduction, Judith Trowell raises the question of what Winnicott means by "management". She goes on to illustrate, through some cases, the importance of fathers, and then comments on some of the benefits of a therapeutic residential setting, where there are a range of possible relationships on offer.

While I agree with all the points that she makes, I would go further. I think that what is striking about the cases she describes is not just the characters and qualities of the mothers and fathers seen as individuals, but the nature of their relationships to one another, and what kind of system is created by this relationship for the children who rely on them. That is, the children have a transference to the family system, to its implicit rules and values, not just to the individual mother and father that gave birth to them.

This is illustrated by the letter quoted in the introduction: the young man who writes with such anger and contempt to a senior politician is attacking not just a father figure but a whole system of government, which he feels to be unjust and corrupt. Similarly, the eleven year-old boy who drew an underwater scene filled with sharks and electric eels, is describing a dangerous world without any benign authority. For the tiny male figure trapped in the tentacles of an octopus, escape from the octopus could only mean destruction by the sharks or the eels: out of the frying pan into the fire.

The exception she referred to is of a young man whose father was in prison, but who encouraged his son to work hard, go to boarding school, and get a good education. In that instance, the father did not just provide something as an individual: he endorsed a whole system. He made it clear that he regretted his own mistakes, the fight with authority that had led him to prison; and that he did not wish his son to continue the fight. Instead, he encouraged him to make a positive transference to a boarding school and an educational system that he believed could be relied upon to reward and protect his son in return for the boy's commitment and hard work. None of the other fathers in Judith Trowell's examples have this kind of faith in a just system.

So I believe that these children need to experience something more than benign individuals: they need to gain some faith in the possibility of a benign system. This is why individual psychotherapy is not enough for them. Their mistrust of the systems adults create through their relationships with one another is projected into any family that tries to foster them, into any school that tries to teach them, and into the professional networks that attempt to look after them. It is only through exposure to a transparently benign system that can withstand these projections that young people from such dysfunctional families can begin to make use of the opportunities of individual relationships.

But it is a difficult job to create a benign system in the face of these children's projections. Before I started to work as a consultant to residential homes and therapeutic communities I worked for several years as a child psychotherapist at a boys' EBD boarding school (EBD = Emotional and Behavioural Difficulties). I consulted to individual staff—anyone who wanted to talk to me about the children, about themselves, and about one another—and had once-weekly sessions with a series of teenage boys who regularly kicked me, tried to strangle me, or brought knives into the sessions. I had one or two successes, but on the whole the results were not encouraging: the work was too slow and too frightening, for the boys and for me. Most of these boys ended up in prison, or disappeared from view. This was despite the hard work of teachers and care staff who, as individuals, were unquestionably benign in their wish to provide something helpful for the children. But the boys were only too aware, as was I, of the embittered relationships and long-standing feuds that existed between various adults and groups of adults. Individuals tried hard, but the system as a whole let everyone down. I have evolved a different way of working over the years, as consultant child psychotherapist in other settings: fostering agencies, therapeutic communities, residential schools, and children's homes.

An illustrative example: Hillingcombe

Hillingcombe can be taken as an illustrative example. Its purpose is to provide residential placements for a group of very disturbed boys and girls between the ages of twelve and eighteen, who are at least as difficult to manage as the boys in the EBD school. Here I never work directly with the children. Instead, my job is helping to facilitate the creation of a psychodynamic thinking space for everyone in the unit. So Hillingcombe operates rather like an ongoing group relations conference, facilitated by staff who are trained and supervised within the child psychotherapy, group relations, and family therapy traditions.

In other words, the adults are expected to do the same intensive work of self-exploration that is expected from the young people who live there, and parallel structures of group and individual forums are provided for both adults and children. All the adults attend regular groups, from the director to the cook and the cleaner. They are expected to use these groups to think together about their own family backgrounds and their relationships to one another, as well as their relationships with the children, using this learning experience to facilitate the children's parallel explorations, and make sense of the dynamics they observe within the children's groups, the children's families, and their own families.

The residential care staff work in fixed teams, on a regular rolling rota, each being run by a male/female pairing. Within these teams, the adults work on their transference relationships to their team leaders, and help one another to observe how they unconsciously replicate the scenarios that existed within their own families. This requires considerable courage and trust: the act of daring to explore negative feelings about themselves and their families, about one another, about the children, and about their own managers at work, in a group setting, can be very exposing. It requires stamina and insight in the team leaders, too, who have to face regular painful criticism of their capacity to parent their team members. It means that they have to work hard to avoid being split into one good parent and one bad parent, and work out together which elements of praise and criticism are justified and which are more to do with the child's inner world. It is no easy task to combine firm management with understanding: but that is what the senior staff try to provide for their junior staff, and what the keyworkers try to provide for the children.

The children's groups are run entirely by the staff. The children have regular community meetings, small group meetings, and a regular boys' group and girls' group run by the male staff and female staff, respectively. They have regular individual meetings with their keyworkers, who also participate in family meetings when the children's circumstances make this possible. I attend one community meeting a week as an observer, read the children's files, and meet with the group leaders to think about their group-work, but I have no other direct contact with the children, except when they come up to me in the corridors to explain that I haven't been giving enough attention to one of their keyworkers, who they think is struggling, or to worry that I've been too harsh on someone, because they saw her crying as she came out of a staff dynamics meeting.

At the end of each week I would meet with the director and his deputies to pool our experiences, and try to make sense of the feelings and fantasies that are whizzing around in the community, in relation to the current events in the adult group and the children's group and as a consequence of our relationships with one another and our impact on the community as a whole.

Unsurprisingly, given a group of adolescent boys and girls, we find ourselves putting a great deal of thought into fantasies around gender. We find that we struggle all the time against the pressure to polarize and typecast men and women. Men and boys get to be bad: delinquent, violent, or incompetent; meanwhile, women and girls get cast as basically good: hard-working and willing, but also weak and hysterical and sometimes crazy.

In their case notes, the mothers are typically described as loving but passive, the victims of drugs and alcohol, the victims of domestic abuse or of a paedophile partner, well-meaning but unable to set boundaries; whilst the fathers are seen as irredeemably selfish, irresponsible, delinquent, perverse, violent, or aggressive.

Put crudely, this description is usually the result of a dynamic where mothers try to get their needs met through mutual idealization with their babies, in what I call a narcissistic dyad. Any negative feelings are projected beyond the dyad into fathers, the extended family, social workers, and the rest of the world. This can seem to result in a loving relationship between mother and baby, but it is entirely suffocating and precludes the development of a more separate identity on either side. As this need for individuation asserts itself, the relationship between mother and child breaks down. Mothers have left their babies with a friend or neighbour, turned to drink or drugs, or to other sexual relationships. They have given up on one infant as he or she begins to individuate, and become pregnant with a new baby who could, for a few months, meet their needs uninterruptedly. Sometimes they have themselves become straightforwardly sadistic to their babies; more often they have provoked or condoned punitive behaviours from fathers, stepfathers, older siblings, or babysitters. You will find examples of these behaviours in the scenarios that Judith Trowell has described in her introduction.

In circumstances like these, individuation becomes extremely dangerous for the baby. It leads to dire consequences—punishment or abandonment. So such babies are trapped "between the devil and the deep blue sea" (Sprince, 2009): a reckless and dangerous individuation, which at a fantasy level—and sometimes in fact—involves sadism towards mother and exposure to a terrifying world; or submission to a relationship with mother that requires the abjuration of any growing sense of individuation, any thinking, any personal autonomy—a relationship of total masochism. Refusing to submit to any external authority therefore becomes an act of extreme personal heroism in the service of sanity.

In individual psychotherapy, the therapist can all too easily become the octopus mother, or can experience herself as the child in the grip of such an octopus. This was the kind of relationship that I had experienced regularly with the boys at the EBD school. Alone with them in the consulting room I would often feel menaced out of any possibility of thinking. Surviving as myself in each encounter with them felt like an act of heroism. Sometimes I succeeded in feeling separate but attuned to a child, and able to make an interpretation that allowed us both to individuate. But then the child would often abandon me, running out of the room or climbing out of the window. I often experienced this as behaviour designed to safeguard us both: the interpretation was helpful, and allowed them to escape, but the very act of attunement defined me as an octopus mother. If they stayed alone with me, it was usually to attack me. The only way through was by means of my own good relationships with the individual staff members who cared for the child, and some kind of triangulation that guaranteed my good faith.

But triangulation with the teachers or care staff was hard to achieve: they experienced the menace, too, and most of them wanted to keep a safe distance. They tended to retreat into strict boundary-setting, and preferred to leave me to deal with the emotions on my own. As I have said, given the provision of only once-weekly therapy this did not lead to speedy improvement: where I managed to create some triangulation with a friendly or sympathetic staff member, the boys did improve—but very, very slowly.

The infantile need to create a split between the qualities of differentiation and attunement, and to attribute these qualities to caricatures of male and female, is hard to resist. I think it finds its way into most family dynamics. This is why the capacity of parents to stay joined together, and to marry these qualities in themselves as individuals as well as in their functioning as a couple, is so important to their children. Where this hasn't happened, the quality of attunement can come to seem monstrous in itself. That is the case for these children, for whom empathy can feel like the prelude to seduction into a corrupt and mad-making relationship.

The quest for individuation and the riddle of the Sphinx

I think that a careful reading of the Oedipus myth draws attention to this internal-world fantasy of a monstrous mother in the early phase that precedes the full Oedipal conflict: although in this version the monster is not an octopus.

Oedipus leaves home because he has been told by the oracle at Delphi that he is fated to kill his father and marry his mother. He doesn't know that he was adopted as an infant by the couple he believes to be his parents. He travels to Thebes, unaware that this is the city where he was born, the only son of the King and Queen, Laius and Jocasta. As he approaches Thebes, Oedipus encounters the Sphinx. She is a creature formed of a combination of parts: behind the face and breasts of a beautiful woman she conceals the haunches of a savage lion. In addition, she has the powerful wings of an eagle, and can fly away whenever she wishes. The Sphinx—whose name means "suffocation"—has been terrorizing the kingdom of Thebes for some time, posing a riddle to all passers-by. When they fail to answer it she strangles and devours them.

Her riddle is not in fact so very difficult to answer: What creature speaks with one voice, but walks on four feet at morning, two at noon, and three at night? Oedipus is the first to guess correctly that this is a man: a baby first, crawling on all fours—someone's son; an adult next, standing on two feet—someone's partner; and then an old man, walking with a stick—someone's father. Thus Oedipus demonstrates that he is able to differentiate between the generations, and know what is appropriate for different roles and stages of life.

The Sphinx, then, is a version of the needy mother I have tried to describe. She inflicts on her victim babies a one-to-one encounter which is terrifying and prevents individuation. Those whom she entraps are seduced by her feminine beauty, her lovely face and breasts. But they are then unable to learn to think, to penetrate her mysteries, to distinguish what is appropriate to the different roles of child, partner, and parent. In this way they are swallowed up and lose their separate identity. Her apparent power disguises a terrible vulnerability: when her riddle is guessed and her victim insists on individuation she leaps off the edge of a cliff and kills herself.

You may wonder why King Laius and Queen Jocasta have found the riddle of the Sphinx impossible to solve. The answer lies in an earlier episode of the story, one less well known within the psychoanalytic tradition. As a young man, and a refugee, Laius had acted as tutor to a little boy, the son of a neighbour and ally who had taken him in as a guest. He became attracted to the boy, abducted him and raped him. The boy subsequently died (Graves, 1960, p. 110). Because of this crime, the gods had forbidden Laius to have children.

This story sets the Theban Royal Family within a scenario familiar to anyone who works with looked after children: Jocasta has knowingly married Laius, a Schedule One sex offender, become pregnant by him, and then collaborated with him in abusing and abandoning the baby— exposing him on the mountain side to be devoured by wild beasts. In forbidding Laius to have children the gods were acting, you might say, in the role of responsible social workers. Jocasta's behaviour suggests that she had no greater understanding than he did of appropriate roles and boundaries. The Delphic prophecy—that Oedipus was destined to kill his father and marry his mother—addresses the likelihood of severe emotional damage to any children brought up by Laius and Jocasta.

Oedipus is able to defeat the Sphinx because he was rescued by a kindly shepherd and brought up not by his birth parents but by adoptive parents who have equipped him with the capacity to develop a separate, independent identity: to individuate. However, his adoptive parents have failed to think through with him the trauma of his infancy and as a result he is split off from his early experiences and has no insight into how they have affected him. He cannot therefore deal successfully with the Oedipal situation—in the sense that we understand the term nowadays.

This is obviously true in a concrete sense—he does not know who his birth parents are, and cannot protect himself from acting-out his Oedipal wishes. However, it is true in another sense as well: he does not seem able to question the symbolic meaning of his actions, or even to be ordinarily curious: he makes nothing of the fact that he has killed a man who is of an age to be his father without discovering who he is; that he has married the widowed Queen Jocasta who is of an age to be his mother. When a plague of infertility later inflicts the kingdom, he is told that it is because Thebes is harbouring the murderer of Laius. Despite being warned not to pursue the matter, he does not consider the possibility that he may be the perpetrator. His lack of insight into his own possible culpability is matched by Jocasta's deliberate avoidance of the truth.

Jocasta's part in the tragedy has usually been overlooked. Again, for anyone used to working with looked after children and their families, she is a familiar figure: the victim child-mother who attracts equivocal sympathy, while Laius, the sexually abusive husband, is universally denigrated and Oedipus, the son, is regarded with horrified pity. Her status as victim disguises her collusive role. As well as marrying Laius in the first place, and conniving at his abuse of their son, Jocasta has wilfully ignored what should have been obvious to her—the possible identity of her second husband. Despite being well aware of the terms of the prophecy, she marries a man young enough to be her son, whose arrival coincides with the death of her previous husband. In a transmuted, hidden form, she is another version of the Sphinx: she allows Oedipus to combine the roles of son and husband, and in the service of her own needs she tries to prevent him from exploring who he really is or from learning the full truth about his history or her own. When the riddle of Oedipus' identity is revealed, like the Sphinx, she kills herself. In comparison with the monstrous Sphinx, Jocasta seems a merely pitiable character. Oedipus colludes with this view, failing to notice Jocasta's similarity to the Sphinx and taking full blame for the guilt of their joint actions. He blinds himself with a pin from her dress and goes into exile. His sons by Jocasta are left to rule Thebes, but instead of collaborating, they lead rival gangs in warfare and almost destroy the City of Thebes, fighting one another to the death. And so the saga continues.

The story of Oedipus, then, is part of a much longer story that describes dysfunction within the kingdom of Thebes throughout many generations. This too is familiar as a theme at Hillingcombe.

The children who are referred likewise come from families with a history of entrenched generational dysfunction. Like Oedipus, many of them have been removed at an early age, but not usually into one stable adoptive placement, as Oedipus was. Instead they often arrive with a bewildering chronology involving multiple placements. Some went into foster care in toddlerhood, some at a later age. Sometimes they were adopted at four or five years of age. Many of them have little recollection of their birth parents; some of them are still in regular contact. But most of them struggle, I think, with the consequences of an internalized Sphinx mother, a mother like the Jocasta who married Laius, and then went on to marry Oedipus.

The consequences of this internalization are manifold. First and most importantly, the early experience of their mother's intense attunement, when it was available, leaves them with something of a sense of hope in the possibility of good relationships. However, the breaks in continuity of placement, and the lack of any adult who can be relied on to give a clear and experiential account of their lives, leaves them deprived of a narrative thread through which to make sense of who they are—of their conscious and unconscious memories. Like Oedipus, they feel a desperate need to know the full story if they are to take complete and creative possession of their internal kingdom. But developmentally they are still at a stage where they need to struggle to achieve their right to personal individuation.

Alongside all of this, their experience of a Sphinx-mother makes them vulnerable to projections: an attentiveness to the needs of others and a denial of their own identities has been their only means of holding on to survival. They live in an internal world in which the rules demand that one seduces and is seduced as a means of exploitation of and by others. Survival has depended on a form of love enforced by terror. This love feels both real and unreal: real because mother had strong and genuinely positive feelings for them as babies; unreal because her love met her own needs rather than theirs. Their feelings of concern are therefore compromised: being "good" means sacrificing the demands of their own internal world, their rights to a mind of their own. It implies a preparedness to deny their own feelings in order to placate a tyrannical internal object, to subscribe to the rules of a corrupt regime, and ultimately to submit to extinction. Being "good"—that is, conforming—can therefore be experienced as being cowardly and inauthentic. Attunement—and therefore femininity—is deeply suspect.

This makes loving dependency on any adult—or, indeed, on any intimate relationship—extremely dangerous. A caricature of differentiation—the constant refusal of empathic attunement—feels the only safe and honest option. It is heroic to rebel, to be delinquent, to be ruthless.

For reasons of space I do not intend to explore fully how this is played out amongst the girls, but I'd just like to observe how much the possibility of pride in their femininity is contaminated by their iden-tification with a mother whose apparent love is secretly self-serving. One sees very clearly how their more ordinary delinquency is varied with seductive and controlling behaviours, over-sugary attempts to be "maternal" towards one another and the younger children, the projec-tion of violence and sadism into the boys, and episodes of savage self-harming. Like Jocasta, too, they see in boys and men either an abusive Laius or a pitiable little boy Oedipus. As a consequence, men and boys are regarded with fear and hatred, or else held in total contempt. In all this they demonstrate the patterns of relating that typify the Sphinx/ Jocasta mother.

Meanwhile, the boys seek refuge in heroic delinquency, and the safety of numbers that can be found in a gang. As one boy said: "I don't know why, and I don't want it to be like this, but being with the gang and hit-ting someone feels wonderful. Like, it's a much better feeling than the idea of having sex with the most beautiful girl in the world." Like ter-rorists, or members of an underground resistance cell, these boys feel, in a way that they cannot articulate, that their delinquency constitutes a courageous struggle for freedom against an evil adult regime.

Heroic delinquency: the case of Tommy

I will illustrate this with a more detailed discussion of a boy I will call Tommy.

When we first met Tommy he was twelve years-old. He was a charm-ing, cheeky little boy, strikingly good-looking, with big brown eyes and a mop of curly black hair. His birth mother had had a history of drug and alcohol abuse, and had had several other children taken away from her. According to the notes in Tommy's file, she had seemed to love her little boy, and had fought to keep him. Tommy and his elder brothers were taken away when Tommy was eighteen months old, then returned for a while, then taken away again. After a drawn-out series of court cases, Tommy was cleared for adoption. By this time, mother had had another two babies. Tommy was eventually placed with a professional couple who adopted him when he was five. His brothers had been too old to find adoptive placements, and were in long-term foster care. The babies were still with mother at the time of Tommy's adoption.

Graham and Diana, his adoptive parents, told us that they were so pleased that they "wouldn't have to cope with the nappy stage": that they had wanted a boy because they were both sporty, and had imagined teaching Tommy to play tennis and cricket. At first they had thought of suggesting that they offer a home to his older brothers as well: but Tommy's social worker told them that these older boys had "attachment issues". She said that they had been very aggressive towards Tommy, and that it was thought best for Tommy to be adopted on his own.

But from the first day, things had gone wrong: Tommy was much more demanding than Diana had anticipated. She had taken time off work, but she acknowledged that she was only too relieved when she could go back to her job and send Tommy to nursery school. The demands of her career, and of Graham's, meant that sometimes both parents needed to be out till late on business, but at these times Tommy's adoptive grandmother, who lived nearby, would come and babysit. However, that arrangement soon broke down. Tommy's grandmother decided to retire to the South of France when Tommy was six, and the couple were left without any family backup in the area.

By the time we became acquainted with Tommy, the adoption had all but broken down. Both at school and at home Tommy was quite unmanageable, and seemed emotionally inaccessible. Wherever he went Tommy was always surrounded by a gang of delinquent boys. Sometimes he was their victim, sometimes their leader. When he was their victim, they would pursue him to his home and throw stones through the windows, and his adoptive mother would call the police. At other times, the police would be called to investigate Tommy's assaults on property and on other boys. Within weeks of his arrival at Hillingcombe, gangs began to form around him, at first to bully him, then to follow his lead. The most consistent manifestation was a gang with Tommy at its centre which tormented the domestic ladies at every opportunity and taunted the maintenance men. This particularly bothered the maintenance team, because they were not allowed to intervene: they did not have the necessary restraint training to meet Ofsted regulations, so they felt they were left to stand there, looking as if they didn't care about protecting the female staff. Meanwhile, Tommy would try to attach himself to the young men on the staff, and would have conversations with them about how women were "only good for one thing".

As we got to know Tommy better we got a clearer sense of what had gone on within his adoptive family. It wasn't just amongst other little boys that he had created a gang mentality: he had attempted to do the same thing with his adoptive father, Graham, and with his father's friends. Graham and his colleague, Geoffrey, would take Tommy with them when they went clay pigeon shooting. The men at the shooting club made a lot of fuss over Tommy, and he loved it; and at first Graham was proud of being able to show him off. But gradually things had got more difficult at home. Tommy seemed to enjoy winding his mother up; he seemed to have a knack of breaking things as if by accident—but Diana was sure it was on purpose, and done to annoy and intimidate her. His behaviour caused an ever-widening split between Diana and Graham. Tommy would refuse to obey his mother, or would deny that he was responsible for something that had gone missing, or got damaged, or destroyed. He would give Graham a mischievous, sidelong grin, and Graham would stand up for him, and make excuses for him. Sometimes, Graham would seem to side with Diana, but give Tommy a secret wink to convey that they both knew that mum was being "a bit over the top". Diana would become increasingly hysterical: she told us that her GP had had to prescribe tranquilizers for her. She would threaten to leave Graham, or would take time off work for stress and retire to bed, leaving Graham to cope with Tommy alone.

The situation became increasingly untenable. Graham could cope with Tommy at weekends, when he could take him out and buy treats for him, but, in the long run, he also found himself incapable of controlling him, despite a strict system of rewards and punishments. Indeed, all the increasingly punitive attempts at boundary-setting imposed by home or school only made matters worse. Tommy's referral to Hillingcombe was Graham's compromise solution: he did not want to end the adoptive placement, but he didn't know what more he could do. Meanwhile, Diana busied herself with her career, and had little to do with Tommy—and not much to do with Graham, either.

At Hillingcombe the group of adults and children were eventually able to help Tommy to think about the loss of his birth mother and his siblings. We wondered whether, like many of our children's mothers, his mother had needed a baby's attentive adoration, but had not been able to cope when each in turn began to develop his own personality through ordinary naughtiness. Perhaps it was at those times that she turned to drugs and/or alcohol, or had become pregnant with another baby. Whether or not this was the case, we thought that Tommy had experienced these periods of abandonment as punishments for his attempts at individuation. Maybe he experienced his older brothers' aggression as a further punishment meted out by the gang of which his mother was the boss. It must have been a relief to Tommy to find himself in a home where he could attach himself to a father who seemed to enjoy his naughtiness, and understand the need to be mischievous. But in this new home, both his grandmother and his mother had punished his naughtiness with abandonment, just as his birth mother had done.

So Tommy chose to attach himself to Graham and his friends, and to turn them into a gang who—in his mind, anyway—despised and hated women.

It was perhaps unfortunate that Tommy was adopted by a couple who came from very traditional backgrounds. Although Diana was a modern career woman, Graham left her to be responsible for the home, and had little to do with the housework. Diana employed domestic help, and did all the cooking herself at weekends, storing the week's meals in the freezer. Tommy found himself joining a male group that could easily seem to hold women in contempt. It suited Tommy to exacerbate this split: he could feel himself to be his father's son, without having to challenge his internal loyalty to his birth mother and her gang. And he could inflict on his adoptive mother all the anger he felt, but could not own, towards the birth mother who had deserted him. What he needed was for Graham and Diana to understand his dilemma, and support one another in demonstrating to him the possibility of a mutually supportive couple: a couple who could make sense together of his early experiences, and understand why he behaved as he did. But to be able to do so they would have had to withstand the powerful effect of the feelings disowned by him and projected into them.

We had some long conversations with Diana: her own childhood had not been easy. Her father had left her mother when she was a baby. Her mother had never re-partnered, although she had been very preoccupied with a series of boyfriends. Diana said her mother had much preferred men to women, and boys to girls. Her older brother had always been her mother's favourite. Diana had defiantly become a professional, a high-flier, but we felt that her competitive feelings towards her own older brother, and her own feelings of deprivation and self-doubt, meant that she was often unsympathetic and secretly contemptuous towards Graham, and could not easily cope with Tommy's hatred, contempt, and rejection.

As a little girl, Diana had experienced her mother and brother as ganging up against her: no wonder she felt so hurt and angry when Graham and Tommy seemed to do the same. She retaliated through retreating into her own world and that, of course, only served to confirm Tommy's belief in the kind of relationship she would require of him, if he were to engage in one at all: a relationship to gratify her own needs, not to meet his.

So Tommy treated her—and all females—with contempt, and then complained at their neglectful treatment of him. Meanwhile, his behaviour to men implied that any male who wanted to protect women was a quisling, a cowardly collaborator within a corrupt regime. If they were real men, they would prove it by joining him in his heroic struggle.

This was a state of mind with which Graham was familiar. Graham had been sent to boarding school at the age of seven: like Tommy, he had felt abandoned, and had been bullied by older boys. He had learned to cope, he told us, by "joining the gang". When he grew up he had got a job in the City. He wasn't really used to women, he said. Diana had been his first ever long-term girlfriend. They had never had a very close relationship, he told us: they were neither of them great talkers and did not live in each other's pockets. They each liked doing their own thing. But they had enjoyed doing things together, and they had hoped that a child would bring them closer. But he now realized that this was a mistake: Diana wasn't cut out to be a mother. He told us in confidence that there were times when he thought that Diana was "a bit loopy, really— she goes doolally at times".

It seemed to us that Tommy's presence had exacerbated in each of his adoptive parents a huge contempt for the opposite gender.

It was fortunate that the staff were able to engage Graham and Diana in a few conversations that helped us all to understand what had gone so wrong. However, once Tommy was out of the house, they had returned to a much more comfortable relationship to one another. They were also very able to understand, from their own experiences, how terrible it was for Tommy to lose them both, when he had no other family, and they were prepared to have him back for the occasional weekend visit.

But they were adamant that they did not want Tommy to live with them ever again.

It was hard for Tommy to believe that Graham had defected. For a long time, he held on to the belief that Graham was secretly on his side, part of his gang, and that he wanted to take him back, but was just too scared of what Diana would say or do.

Many boys come to Hillingcombe with a similar conscious or unconscious hatred and mistrust of women, and an open or secret contempt for men who protect them or partner with them. However, both the staff and residents at Hillingcombe have a long-standing familiarity with such patterns of thinking, and the behaviour that follows from it, and the children joined with the adults in addressing with Tommy his difficulty in believing that men and women could join together in an equal and helpful way, and use their partnerships to give children the love and understanding that they need. They pointed out to Tommy how he replayed, over and over again, the scenario of his early childhood, where his mother insisted on enlisting him into her gang to fight against people who were trying to look after him, even though her actions exposed him to neglect and bullying.

Over his first eighteen months, as he began to understand his own part in what happened around him, and how it deprived him of the possibility of being close to anyone, Tommy started for the first time to put real effort into his relationship with his adoptive mother. After he had been at Hillingcombe just over a year, he decided to ask Diana to take him shopping for his new football kit. This was an unprecedented event. It went along with a diminution of his delinquent behaviours. What followed, however, was a long period of deep depression, and new feelings of agonizing jealousy: Tommy was sure that his keyworker would prefer other children to him; that he could never become a man that any woman would want as a partner; that everyone hated him, and would always do so.

For Tommy, the gang, with its manic delinquency, its disparagement of dependency, and its lack of differentiation, had protected him from experiencing the full struggle of Oedipal jealousy. At Hillingcombe he watched with eagerness and fascination the intimate pairings between male and female staff, through which they ran their teams, worked collaboratively and intensively with the children, and helped one another to think about the community's dynamics. He began to wonder whether

Graham and Diana might be capable of a more equal and mutually dependent relationship than he had suspected and whether there might be something authentic in Graham's decision that his relationship with Diana was more important to him than his relationship to Tommy and the gang. He became obsessively attached to his maths teacher who had recently become engaged, and questioned her about her future plans for a family.

I think Tommy's feelings of depression were not only the result of loss; they were the result of a development in his internal world of a new kind of conscience, which helped him to feel appropriately guilty about his attempts to divide his adoptive parents, and manipulate his father into attacking his mother. One might describe it as a change of inner-world constitution: Tommy began to believe in the possibility of a collaborative democracy, rather than a corrupt dictatorship. This, in turn, gave him some real hope that he could be helped to become himself and get his own voice heard through some means other than terrorism.

It is possible that Tommy might have achieved this progress through intensive individual therapy, supported by family work, couple work, or individual therapy for his parents. However, I think that Tommy's difficulties would have made him deeply suspicious of any one-to-one relationship—particularly with a female therapist. My own experience of working as a psychotherapist with such children leads me to think that this would have taken more years than were available for Tommy before he reached adulthood. Moreover, I doubt whether his adoptive parents would have engaged in anything more than a very superficial exploration of the part played by their own dynamics in Tommy's difficulties. They did not feel that they were to blame for Tommy's delinquency. Nor indeed were they, except insofar as their ordinary decency offered Tommy enough hope of rescue to dare to be delinquent.

The problem they faced as adoptive parents was not peculiar to them. Children like Tommy regularly subject parental figures to intense and attentive intuitive scrutiny: they have been trained to do so from babyhood. They demand from them a far higher degree of insight than is demanded from ordinary, good-enough parents, and in addition a willingness to make extraordinarily fine and careful judgements about what feelings belong to whom and what do not. Only through such means extended over time do children like Tommy begin to trust that they are not being tricked into corrupt relationships, to subscribing to the corrupt laws of a self-serving tyranny, but are rather being helped to establish within themselves an autonomous but collaborative conscience.

Tommy's ability to stay, at least some of the time, with depression, and with the terrible feelings of loss, betrayal, and guilt, depended fundamentally on an adult group that could empathize with his predicament, and on a children's group that understood the importance of not allowing him to slip back into a gang mentality. This in turn depended upon the psychoanalytic insight available to everyone within the community, all of the time. Restraining Tommy when he tried to hurt people or when he smashed the windows went side-by-side with talking to him about why he was doing it—conversations in which both adults and children participated.

I have used Tommy as an example of many children who go through Hillingcombe with a similar positive outcome: with educational outcomes often far exceeding the national average for looked after children, holding responsible jobs—in some cases in the caring professions, and staying in touch.

Perhaps the most gratifying outcome is when ex-residents ring up to discuss with staff their ongoing problems as partners or parents. In the texture and content of their conversations, they display an insight, a thoughtful attentiveness, and a willingness to accept their own contribution to their children's difficulties that give me huge hope for their children's future lives, as well as for their own.

References

Graves, R. (1960). *Complete Greek Myths*. London: Penguin Books.

Sprince, J. (2009). "The devil and the deep blue sea": Dyadic narcissism and the problem of individuation. *Journal of Child Psychotherapy, 22(1):* 13–31.

Trowell, J. & Etchegoyen, A. (Eds.) (2001). *The Importance of Fathers*. London: Routledge.

Winnicott, D. W. (1956). The Antisocial Tendency. In: *Through Paediatrics to Psychoanalysis* (pp. 306–315). London: Hogarth Press.

Society and the antisocial tendency: "physician, heal thyself!"

Richard Rollinson

Setting the scene

This being the last lecture in this series, I am aware you do not need telling, or even reminding, about Winnicott and the antisocial tendency. Therefore, I shall operate here as "the Fifth Business", to take a phrase from the celebrated novel by Robertson Davies (1970)—that is, as the one whose role in a drama is supposedly that of being neither Hero nor Heroine, Confidante nor Villain, but still essential for the dénouement of the plot. In this guise I plan to speak in rather extempore fashion in a way I hope Winnicott himself would approve of. I shall play around with a number of important ideas about young people and society from his times and his perspective as a way of tackling some serious current issues in our own.

A very different world from ours?

Dr. Winnicott delivered his paper, "The Antisocial Tendency", fifty-four years ago on 20 June 1956 before the British Psychoanalytic Society. What else was happening during that year?

In no particular order of significance:

I was seven years of age and a New Yorker. That was my world, *the* world as far as I was concerned.

- It was a Leap Year.
- The film, *The Wizard of Oz*, was televised for the very first time, and certainly not the last!
- The play, *West Side Story*, by Bernstein and Sondheim, was produced for the stage.
- The first IBM hard drive was developed, twenty miles from where I lived.
- James Dean starred posthumously in the film, *Rebel Without a Cause*. It was released in November 1955 but was distributed in January 1956. Hence over long years the nickname "56 Gang" came to be employed popularly to identify real and "wannabe" bikers.
- And Billy Dougherty, my sixteen year-old next door neighbour, was serenaded each summer night by his gang who hooted under his window, "Wilbur's tied to his mother's apron strings!", for which mother cursed them loudly before they roared off to commit mayhem.
- It was a presidential election year: war hero Eisenhower *vs.* patrician diplomat Adlai Stevenson. I was introduced to the Cold War while playing in the park. Older boys were arguing, one saying that if Eisenhower won, half the world would be destroyed by fire; the other insisting that if Stevenson won, half the world would freeze. In the face of such informed political debate (which, I now realize, was not far off the level of adult discourse at that time!) I was frightened and thought: "What! How can that be fair, either way?!"

As you will readily appreciate, my context and memories are mid-century American ones, whereas yours almost certainly are not. But that is not important. In the society of the post-war 1950s, on both sides of the Atlantic, everyone knew their place—hot or cold—or so it is supposed. It still felt like a long time to the 1960s when JFK would be proclaiming in his inaugural address: "The world is very different now." From my standpoint, more than half a century on, I would say that the world is always different. In 1956 many more people married when starting a family, and less than 2% divorced. Now, as I write this, two-thirds of children starting nursery/pre-school in September will not be living in the same family by the age of sixteen. That's different.

I will not say if it is better or worse; just that it's different, and will be different again, fifty years on.

Getting the measure of ourselves: a mature society?

Winnicott (1963) asked whether our society was strong enough, healthy enough, to tolerate antisocial behaviour and recognize, receive, and manage its younger citizens into the social and civic world. Clare Winnicott stated in her introduction to her husband's *Deprivation and Delinquency* (1984): "[T]he practical question is how to maintain an environment that is humane enough and strong enough to contain all, even those who may then be bent on destroying it" (p. 5).

On that measure how are we doing today? What are we doing in society to meet the challenge and to answer Winnicott's question—fifty-four years after he wrote his paper "The Antisocial Tendency", forty-seven years after "Struggling through the doldrums", and forty-three years after "Delinquency as a sign of hope"?

Let's look honestly at our performance as he would expect us to do.

In important ways, and again not listed in any rank order of priority:

- *We diminish and degrade public spaces for other purposes*

We privatize some areas, abandon others, and oversee many more with an undemocratic zeal and a disregard for people that we used to impute to Iron Curtain regimes. In particular, we restrict child and young person access to these areas by various "devices" including the current high-pitch sound emitters intended to drive groups away. Out of fear, parents can contribute to this public disapproval of their presence, often tightly controlling where their children can go.

Shopping malls and NHS Trust facilities send out their own unwelcoming messages to the young. Yet it is in public places, in group interactions, that children and young people learn, practice, make some mistakes and "get it" in other ways as they take on their more social roles unsupervised or only loosely so.

- *We criminalize many more behaviours of the young and see them as "bad" already or as heading that way*

If one looks at recent crime statistics: rates of violent crimes against children have risen hugely (Home Office, 2010). *But*, once one removes from that figure those incidents in schools and playgrounds that occur between and amongst young people themselves, then the rate drops by 70%! In the past, except in the most serious cases, these would simply be dealt with as disciplinary issues within school. Nowadays, dealing with such behaviour in situ is not only much less possible or permissible, but even appears less desirable to adults in positions of authority, as well as to many parents. Moreover, other factors enter in and complicate matters of assessment and evaluation. Not long ago police in Cornwall charged a child with twenty-seven separate offences for one incident—to reach performance targets that otherwise would not have been reached.

Winnicott referred to the "total environmental reactions" that are provoked by antisocial behaviour *and* by the absence of sufficient thoughtful public, social, official response. The direction of travel today is clear—towards Blame, Intolerance, and Punishment, or ever more strident demands for punishment.

Anti-Social Behaviour Orders (ASBOs) themselves are not crime records, but breeching them is a crime; and many are "set up" for that to happen, when they are not being embraced as badges of "dishonour" by the young who call the adults' bluff. Trespass is such an easy "crime" for young people to commit now.

On the very first morning of the 2010 election campaign, the Director of an independent think tank was making great play on Radio 4 of the necessity for all political parties to deal firmly with binge-drinking by the young in towns and cities. It must be eliminated; it is intolerable! There was no effort to introduce perspective, proportion, or understanding in order to guide intervention.

On *Question Time*, David Starkey, the historian, was recently to be heard arguing that the current Children's Commissioner, Maggie Atkinson, should be sacked for proposing that the age of criminal responsibility be raised from ten to twelve, adding that 25% of children were "feral" and needed "dealing with". He wasn't a lone public voice!

The two boys under twelve who were tried for raping an eight year-old girl, while acquitted of the most serious charges, were convicted of crimes that put them on the sex offenders register. At the trial's end, the Judge invited comments from any interested parties "on the *process*" of the trial. (*Guardian*, 2010; my emphasis). Well, my comment is on the *fact* that there had been a trial "process" at all. The prosecution, as you would expect, made a highly choreographed presentation of the "evidence" that malignly served to mirror and exacerbate social shock and voyeurism, not least by releasing the photo of the "victim" holding the teddy bear they had got her and which she dubbed "Mr Happy" when coaxed to name him. Overall the process resembled a "show trial". It did nothing either to secure justice, protect children, make communities safer, or support the principals in becoming healthier, wholesome individuals. A trial such as this is more a commentary on our society and its treatment of children (however "antisocial" some might be), than it is an indication of the relentless and sordid rise of feral youth.

There is a saying: "We preach Justice, we crave Mercy, we practice Vengeance." The general "mess making" that Winnicott referred to (1956, p. 311) as an early manifestation of "the antisocial tendency" (and he didn't just mean untidy bedrooms) can easily count as a crime nowadays, with a much reduced response repertoire—"shoplifters are always prosecuted"; "abuse of staff is not tolerated and will always be prosecuted".

I do not suggest there are no real problems, but we need to look honestly at what produces and then sustains them.

- *And when we aren't criminalizing and rendering children "bad",*
  we look to construct them as "mad"/disordered

DSM-5 (Diagnostic and Statistical Manual of Mental Disorders, 5th edition) is due to be published in May 2013; ICD-11 (International Statistical Classification of Diseases and Related Health Problems, 11th Revision) is due from the World Health Organization (WHO) in final form in May 2014. Like its transatlantic counterpart, the new publication is likely to increase its diagnoses and disorders by 20%, as it usually has done with each new "iteration". This is a process Frank Füredi (2003, p. 182) calls "the diseasing of childhood" and Gail McLeod (2010, p. 95) terms "the medicalisation of naughtiness". Visser and Jehan (2009, p. 204) contend that for every child diagnosed as having ADHD (Attention Deficit Hyperactivity Disorder) who may actually have a genuine difficulty in "attending", many, many more are pathologized by those who choose to frame such difficulties within an uncomplicated (and simplistic) biomedical paradigm. Any alternative explanations, and hence recommendations for treatment, are largely discarded.

Winnicott was clear that the antisocial tendency was precisely that—a tendency. It was neither diagnosis nor disorder (1956, p. 308). Without recognition of, and response to it, as such, then a "social disease" of stealing and destruction begins to emerge in society. In our day, through that total environmental reaction, a public health problem is unacknowledged and instead is pushed back on to the child as their personal, private "disorder". It is a tidy inversion, or rather, a perversion, of where both source and solution reside—in relationships or in their absence. The dimension of the antisocial tendency that Winnicott identified as the disposition to behave in defiance of the constraints of society is ignored, as is the sign of hope implicit in that encounter.

- *As a society and not infrequently as individuals, we actively create and encourage antisocial behaviour and then react—stepping back in horror first before moving forward in righteous fury*

Consider the issue of drinking to excess. A large part of the culture and economy of cities and town centres is geared to such excessive consumption, with advertising running unabated. If it really stopped, there would be another economic downturn. Shoplifting similarly—advertising and "disposable money" proclaim the primacy of style—and the absolute need to acquire the most recent clothing, accessories, and electronic gear. If they don't have the money, many young people will tell you that they will secure the newest gadget by hook or crook, rather than be caught with last month's now passé item and risk being rendered "sad" or "3" (that is, DEF—deficient).

- *We use rhetoric and language not to give clear information and invite children's thoughtful engagement and response, but to persuade/ influence them with glitz and shallow words*

Think of the phrase ZERO TOLERANCE of bullying or of the widespread school and workplace policy to "fight bullying". The former term denotes intolerance and will not succeed in containing and transforming bullying or anything else. It simply drives it underground or elsewhere.

As for ourselves, we can be expert in blinding children to reality. A character in a Robertson Davies' novel, *The Manticore* (1972), once observed about adulthood: "How readily the qualities of adult authority and power can be brought to the service of the wildest nonsense and cruelty." There's self-deception—recall the Pythons famous remark: "Oh, Dinsdale, he was cruel … but fair." Then there's deception of others: In the film *Chicago* (Dir. Rob Marshall, 2002) we are presented with a celebrity lawyer, notorious for getting his clients off on charges for which they are transparently guilty, and then a celebrity dancer on trial for murder. She is well and truly "nailed" by the evidence of a witness and the actual "smoking gun". Turning to her lawyer in despair, she asks: "So what do we do now? They've got me." To which he replies: "Well, when there is nothing at all to do about the evidence, the only thing left is—give them the 'Old Razzle Dazzle'." He then breaks into a wonderful four-minute song and dance routine that says in effect: "Don't look over there, at the evidence; look here, here, no—here—at my distracting song and dance." And, of course, she is acquitted!

Is this a case of Art imitating life, or life imitating Art? Indeed, it actually happens. We use our language to block or prohibit conversation and exploration, especially about uncomfortable things—things that we can't really explain or justify, not infrequently about what we ourselves say or do. Consider such well-worn phrases as "I want to draw a line under this incident …"; "Yes, the patient died and that was sad, but the operation itself was a success"; and "I only want their [young people's] respect."

The antisocial tendency that needs to be noticed instead gets NOTICES—"No ball playing. No skateboarding. No bike riding here."; "All violators will be prosecuted."; "Do not …"; "Beware, this is not a public space."; "Beware, this is not a right of way."; "You mind yourself."; "You must …"; "You must not …" In the face of this heavy blast of commands and demands and prohibitions what do the young "own"? And where are they "owned"—outside the home or even in it?

So often do we or our public representatives dissemble in our communications that it is little wonder young people regularly withdraw and are disconnected from state provision and facilities. As part of British Care Leavers' Week in October 2004, the then Social Exclusion Unit (SEU) launched their report on vulnerable young adults and their difficulties in accessing state services. They observed how disconnected were these various services; yet of more interest to them was the revelation (or so it appeared to them) of how disorganized in their thinking were these young adults! I observed to them that there may be a connection that they were missing—namely that the latter—the apparent disorganized thinking of the young adults—is in a fundamental way a function, a necessary function, of the former—the disconnectedness of the various services that should be easily available to them, however disorganized these young adults may be in themselves. They looked startled at my comment.

- *We celebrate wealth and consumption, and privilege the individual over groups and society often to an ostentatious and extreme degree*

The message is clear even to the very young: "There's only Number One. Look after yourself first and always. And if you don't have it in abundance, you are 'less than zero'." This continues to be propagated to this very day, despite a near total economic meltdown, the only prevention of which, we are told (for now), depends precisely upon the ability of people to continue to spend and consume, even while being told of the dangers of excess. It must indeed be easy to be confused as a young person.

Winnicott knew the real difference between greediness and greed. In the antisocial tendency he observes that greediness is a common symptom of that tendency, showing deprivation which can be met and treated; it is not simply greed. In his seeing an aspect of stealing as an unrelenting compulsion to go out and buy things ("retail therapy" today), we can make a link to our adult world, where some don't just compulsively shop and buy. We "borrow" beyond our means; we acquire by leverage; we "steal"—on a grand scale as some banks and businesses have shown—before a few crashed, but many escaped scot-free.

The huge profits made by several major companies post-2008 were due to takeovers of distressed companies for a song. Businesses were bought and the territory cleared. Hence the massive bonuses since January 2010 paid for non-performance "performance". And there are the Great Escapes by RBS, Northern Rock, HBOS executives and numerous others, including some Asset Fund managers, who leveraged many millions of pounds of debt onto their companies and took much of that money immediately as "profits" for themselves and their associates, thereby contributing directly to the 2008 economic downturn with all its consequences for those not so enriched.

Now here's where we need not ASBOs, but ASBBOs—Anti-Social Banker Behaviour Orders, Anti-Social Business Behaviour Orders; or perhaps AMBOs—Asset Manager Behaviour Orders.

But meanwhile the messages to youths continue: "Don't do this"; or, "Always try to do it big!" Shoplifting? "Take a lesson from us, the real winners: take the whole shop, the whole chain! Take, take, take."

- *At the same time we often idealize children and childhood, presenting it as a Golden Age of innocence or of wisdom untainted by adult experiences*

This of course is happening while at the same time TV dramas constantly feature storylines involving the past or current abuse of children. So in one case we have the child as untrammelled; in the other, the child as victim. And these two positions are held simultaneously without apparent discomfort or a feeling of contradiction. The truth is, we prefer our fantasies about children rather than the reality of them.

Consider the last Labour government's major initiative, Every Child Matters (2004). This was their response to the Laming report on the death of Victoria Climbié (2003) with its injunction to him, restated in the report's preamble, to make recommendations for taking "all necessary steps to protect the most vulnerable children in our society". Every Child Matters had been launched as a framework for a comprehensive universal service, bringing together health, education, and social welfare. It is a worthy goal and fine sentiment. Universal services have much to commend them, and as regards Every Child Matters, for the 12,500,000 children currently under the age of sixteen in England and Wales, my experience tells me that:

- Sixty-five per cent (8,125,000) will do very well indeed with what's available in/through this universal service—at home, in school, in the community. They always do.
- Twenty-five per cent (3,125,000) will manage well enough with just a little extra support and attention; and many of them will quickly outgrow any need for this extra provision, too. That's what always happens.

- Six per cent (750,000) will require a much more planned, extensive, and longer term level of support simply to be safe and to manage well enough. But Services can be creative and imaginative in providing this—resources permitting!
- Four per cent (500,000) will represent the most vulnerable, the most at risk, the most complex in their difficulties and their needs, whether because they are socially invisible, like Victoria, or relentlessly "in our face" with their behaviour. Breaking this down further—2.5% (312,500) will really stretch us to reliably identify their needs and meet them with the right set of provisions (in care, education, and health treatment); these are the ones about whom we often are scratching our heads in puzzlement; the other 1.5% (187,500) are those that seem to be at the very limits or beyond our capacity to understand and intervene at all helpfully—a most highly troubled, often chaotic, and not infrequently highly troublesome population of our children and young people with their: severe emotional problems; aggressive, even violent behaviours; self-harming (hurting or killing themselves); little or no sense of self-preservation; and/or being apparently entirely out of control through their uncontainable acting-out of feelings—of anger/rage, anxiety, and distress.

And in a total population of 12,500,000 that means that conservatively, at any one time, there are approximately 250,000 highly troubled/ troublesome, invisible, and desperately vulnerable children. Within a universal framework of provision these are the very ones for whom there is the greatest struggle to access services that will make a genuine difference to their safety and healthy growth and development. Of course, there has been some great protective work that has emerged over recent years, but such interventions have been—and will continue to be—mainly down to individual efforts or those of a small group. Genuine protection for every child is not universally available across Britain. So in our antisocial society the title should more accurately be "Every Child Matters—except for the ones that don't fit neatly into a universal service, who often happen to be the most troublesome and/ or vulnerable".

More careful thought and targeted work is needed to bring the reality of protecting the most vulnerable children in our society beyond simplistic political remedy and pious expressions of good intent. Such unreflective pieties can easily degenerate into sentimental idealization, and then just as easily transform into denigration and demonization once confronted by the reality of real children, especially "troublesome" ones.

- *When not demonizing some children we render them invisible—out on the streets literally, or moving in the shadows on the margins of society*

We sometimes see them around, but in our minds and conversations we are seeing what we want to see and describe; we don't describe what we actually see, or at least not soon enough to make a difference by intervening, responding, and reaching out, as the Winnicotts would expect. Children send up "smoke signals" to alert us to the dangers ahead if we don't respond to them, but we don't notice. The conflagration has to erupt, as antisocial acts—done to elicit limit-setting and social reparation for injustices; it has to get out of hand and become something else—violence or criminal damage—in order for adult horror and rage to take hold. Whereupon, finally, the child becomes visible as real and actual in the person of the young offender.

- *We "worry"*

Even though crime rates, including those involving juveniles, have fallen dramatically over the past decade-plus, we still worry about the danger of becoming a victim: no going out at night into dangerous streets and amongst psychopathic individuals and adolescent hordes. And by this dynamic, which reduces our social presence, we are helping to produce the very things we ostensibly fear.

A significant thing about the word "worry", as the psychiatrist Tom Main (1989) pointed out, is that it has two meanings in English. One is the genuine slightly anxious caring concern; the other "worry" is when an animal, usually a dog, chases and harasses sheep. If not stopped, the dog will continue to "worry" the sheep, snapping at their heels without ceasing, until their hearts give out from panic and exhaustion or they are caught in the wire around the field or they plunge into a river and drown. We can sometimes do the same sort of "worrying" when we believe we are only trying to help. We worry the children and young people relentlessly, and they in turn drive us into ever greater activity to "help" by rebuffing our efforts to sort them out. And we go on and on at them until they evade us, retaliate, or exhaust us—sometimes driving us to actual collapse ourselves!

- *We demand compliance, a state of mind which for Winnicott meant an abandonment of hope of change*

We want "good" children—"If you're not good, you won't …" And we don't want adolescents—we want "adultescents". And those complying have no heart for it, or hope; there's only emptiness. Then, after "heart and hope" have been staunched for a long time, if by chance some hope slips through and gives heart, the emergence of the antisocial behaviour can be intense—like in a revolt from rising expectations. In April 1990 the prisoners in Manchester's Strangeways Prison rioted for 25 days until the site was largely destroyed. Interestingly, this riot began a fortnight after Judge Stephen Tumin, the then Inspector of Prisons, had visited and found that the appallingly dire conditions he'd encountered a year before were much improved, even if there remained much more to do; it was as if a year before there was no hope and compliance was guaranteed. The lesson for us is clear today, too. If we demand compliance alone in our society the bill for payment will come in eventually and powerfully. Deprivation risks becoming Depredation.

- *We "promise" children and young people*

We proffer all sorts of things to secure their accommodation to our wants, to entice them to behave, even to seduce them to misbehave sometimes. Government programmes for work, for learning, for achieving, are launched with much promise—until the delivery on the promises becomes a struggle. Then the programmes are abandoned or turned into something else.

"You can be anything you want to be"; "Everyone's a winner"; "Always follow your dreams"; "Study, choose, work hard—you'll get that job"—these are only slight caricatures of the social message. Yet in reality we can often leave only a scrapheap culture for the non- and under-achievers. And all this is said and done instead of giving an honest message, like: "Try to be the very best you can be at what you find you are good at; develop your strengths—and keep trying."

- *We are "self-absorbed" in our public behaviour and presentation of self*

We barge along pavements and sometimes even drive while talking or "txting" on our mobile—with little or no regard for anyone else, let alone the young! The evidence is everywhere visible in our everyday "social world".

Reflecting on all these things we say and do, a growing child or challenging adolescent could be forgiven for thinking: "What? What are they expecting me to do—as they say or as they do?" It's a fair position, an honest enquiry. After all, who is actually being more antisocial, not just in tendency but in determined effort? Winnicott says that delinquency and the antisocial tendency are signs of hope, but who is responsible today for holding the hope and for trying to understand what can happen when hope, for so long lost, suddenly emerges?

An honest analysis

There is a serious risk here for children and for society, including even those children doing well or well enough. If things cannot shift, the outcome may not be a Strangeways-type "Bang", but nor will it be a whimper. And much "private pain" will become a very transparently public problem.

However we look at it, children and young people in transition are searching for ways of reliably being held in mind—healthily—in a different form and style than in infancy and younger childhood, with a lot more space and "wriggle room" to be oneself and to experiment to find that self—while still contained in and feeling a member of the community.

Either they experience that Healthy Mind, and test it thoroughly, or they will eventually seek elsewhere for an alternative Mind. Christine, aged six, and Roseanne, fourteen, taught me that. Each in her own way told me that she needed to feel held *in* the Mind of caring, concerned people (attachment). If they could not have that, they did all they could to be *on* people's Minds, usually as Problem more than as person (attention). If they were neither in nor on a Healthy Mind they felt not only out of that particular Mind, but *out of* their own Mind, and so acted as madly as they felt or feared themselves to be.

Children such as these, being so intolerably frightened by that lonely, private madness, actively seek out, in adolescence especially, another Mind, any Mind to be in, rather than feel out of theirs. Waiting nearby, inevitably, is the Delinquent Mind of the Margins, the Streets— the shadow world of gangs, crime, drugs (taking, selling, trafficking), sex, violence, etc. And we know from experience that once lost in the grip of such a "Mind" too often there is little or no way back. Or, even if by chance some resist that Delinquent Mind, they are nevertheless stuck in a solitary, past-caring, empty-life Mindlessness—"Don't mind"; no affect.

It is true that some, who have become "lost", are reclaimed actively; some others themselves find a way out and back—remarkably, and usually after many hurts. Yet too many others never emerge from that "Mind". However awful, it is a Mind in which they can belong, and not feel mad, lonely, and scared. The names of some gangs show there is no way back available or sought—"No Name Boys", "Anti Social Rude Boys", "Bombastic Radicals". And even then there are no real group relationships in gangs. All that exists is the highly individualized and controlling contact between a gang leader and each of the gang members. No other "relationships" are tolerated. Should some begin to emerge, the "offending" members are attacked and expelled and/ or harmed. Gangs are not groups; members are effectively "alone in a crowd", and in being so their global condition in a wider, uncaring society is replicated on a local scale.

For societies, if the balance between its healthy and unhealthy "Minds" tips too greatly towards the latter, social life will go on. However, it will be diminished, compromised, and contingent— dominated by arbitrary power, not guided by a healthy authority and contained by boundaries offering the space of genuine belonging while also defining limits that ensure collective security.

What to do, how to understand?

Is it looking difficult for young people? Well, we adults don't have an easy time either—we're not immune ourselves from some of these negative tendencies. And, we're thinking about the antisocial tendency and wondering where we can find pro-social ones. So, we have to consider just how massively different is our society and the world of 1956, my starting point, particularly in respect of our means of communication. By any standards there has been an enormous explosion in the ways of communicating with one another, as well as in the immediacy and pervasiveness of these means. There really has been nothing like such a revolution in communications since the introduction of moveable type printing in late fifteenth-century Europe.

Some adults have taken to the new communication technology "like a duck to water", while others, like myself, only dip a toe into that water or possibly wade out up to our knees. However, what we must recognize is that society for children and young people today has at its heart the internet and social networking—an electronic, virtual, high-speed life. They are leaving us behind in ways at the speed of light. But we are not redundant. There is a vital role for us still—to continue to be available to the young—to be, to represent a "live presence", to support, "to preserve and protect" genuine communication and well-being in, between, and amongst people—beyond Facebook and through to face-to-face, faces-to-faces, in live, real-time human and humane interaction.

Of course, all that was printed in the sixteenth century was not wonderful. Much of it was totally wrong, crazy, and downright dangerous. Today the same is true—in addition to its benefits the internet exports porn, grooming in chatrooms, misinformation disguised as fact or truth, and a range of other misuses of social networks. Just recently the *Guardian* reported the stabbing to death by a young person of a former friend for "dissing" him on Facebook. Networking doesn't ensure healthy communication and mutual regard. We have a duty to try to offer that to children and young people in our interactions and social exchanges with them—actively, with our fantasy fears contained and mindful that we are of relevance.

Will we be hoeing a lonely row?

Now in the midst of all this confusion, risk, and change can Dr Winnicott help us? I believe he can point us in a direction that will help us understand a way forward.

Winnicott gave us this steer by designing his own "X Factor". He set this out in his 1950 paper, "Some thoughts on the meaning of the word democracy". First he gave a working definition of the word "democracy", as "society well-adjusted to its healthy members" (p. 240); that is, a democratic society is mature, it has a quality that is allied to the quality of individual maturity which characterizes its healthy members.

His interest, post-World War II and in the midst of the Cold War, can be expressed in a formula—Democracy = maturity = health, which is desirable; and therefore thought must be given to identifying ways to support the *tendency*.

For Winnicott the X factor is the quantity of individuals in society who show their lack of sense of society by developing an antisocial tendency.

In this society there is also the Z factor—the quantity of individuals who react to inner insecurity by the tendency to identify with authority. This identification does not arise out of self-discovery; it is a "prosocial but anti-individual tendency" that forms a "hidden antisocial" element.

Neither X nor Z factor people are entirely whole and wholesome in themselves.

Then there is the Y Factor—his "Indeterminates", swing voters in the emotional maturity stakes so to speak, who sometimes can act in a mature and healthy way and other times not. The way they "swing" depends upon the extent of maturity they encounter in society. For Winnicott the more mature an element there is in society the greater is the swing of this group towards that democratic tendency. And of course, the less maturity the less the swing.

Therefore, the overall proportion of the Democratic Tendency (DMT) in a society—that is, those reliably mature enough to add a social dimension to their well-grounded personal development and sense of wholeness—can be calculated thus:

DMT = 100 − (X + Y[XZ] + Z), where y[xz] represents the Indeterminates who out of weakness and fear shift to X factor, while DMT includes those y who move to maturity.

Hence if DMT incorporates for Winnicott 30% minimum fully mature and 20% of Indeterminate "Y"s drawn to that position, its 50% proportion offers sufficient innate DMT for practical purposes, and there will be much less risk of "submergence in the antisocial". He advises us to check secure facilities in societies to see when/if there is the emergence of agents of antisocial control. He says that the X factor antisocials are not intrinsically anti-democratic; he is far more wary of the Y factor group due to its tendency when weak and/or fearful to be drawn into association with the antisocial and then along with the Z factor towards the authoritarian that adopts initially a democratic façade for "hoodwinking".

In society, Winnicott insists that all depends on strengthening the Democratic Tendency and avoiding compromising the future by well-intentioned interfering: he favours organized non-interference with ordinary good-enough parents and families; education for emotional maturity; and not imposing democratic machinery on total communities. In effect he says support the emotionally mature and any tendency towards it, and let time do the rest!

By 1956 Winnicott had begun proposing strategies to assist the X factors and the wavering Indeterminates to move towards that Democratic tendency. He always knew society needed as many mature people as it can secure; today we certainly can't turn our backs on any possible member in the pool of democratic maturity. What, then, does he propose we do?

Finding our way

Earlier in this series of Squiggle lectures Adrian Ward spoke on the subject of The Application of the Antisocial Tendency to Residential Care. He identified some important features at the heart of any therapeutic work with children in the context of the daily living of the residential group. Following Winnicott's Democratic Tendency perspective, I have been thinking about the more public dimension of these residential features—in the sense that healthy communities and society have a key group dimension, too. The dimensions I want to consider are:

- Boundaries and Space
- The use of relationships
- The (conscious) use of self
- Tolerance

In reference to the first, it is clear, but appears to require constant restatement, that for society to understand children when they are troublesome does not mean either excusing or passively accepting what they say or do. It does mean being very clear about limits, and about their reasons for existing; and about supporting the spaces defined within those limits to explore freely and even to test the integrity of the limits—of those boundaries and of themselves. To do so offers the opportunity for them to learn from experiences, which as we adults know means making errors and misjudgements sometimes. Any social or community boundaries must make sense and be predictable, while having some flexibility. Young people testify time and again that they struggle most with the unpredictable, with sudden swings between disinterested permissiveness and harsh reaction/retaliation. In a secure unit outside Lisbon some years ago the grounds had only three fences; the other perimeter opened out onto a large, but readily negotiated, downward slope towards the sea. Nevertheless, young people rarely left of their own accord, due to the severe material and social poverty that awaited them if they absconded. The ones who did run off were those who refused to comply with a harsh regime and even challenged it. They were effectively driven out by staff mistreatment.

On the arrival of the new Director who was determined to treat the young people rather than just incarcerate and intimidate them, his first therapeutic action was to order the fourth perimeter to be fenced; only then could the hard work of culture change and growth begin to happen. Our society sometimes risks just as effectively driving out young people from a sense of belonging. Yet it is possible to do things differently.

Regarding relationships, it is an opportunity to get closer to children and young people in easy times and, when things are going wrong, not to blame, but to name and inquire: "You seem to be …"; "You seem to want to …"; "*We* don't do that …"; "What do you think you are trying to do …?"; "What do you think you are trying to say when you …?"—an inclusive asking or telling, not a rhetorical or direct telling off. My experience is that it can and does work, especially when we are in touch sooner rather than later when something has already "kicked off". Try it, even if like me you are grey and somehow invisible to youths unless you make your presence known positively. Penny Nicholls of the Children's Society is of the same view (Nicholls, 2009). Reach out, engage, notice the good, and the boundaries being tested. I am reminded of the book, *The Gift Relationship*, by Richard Titmuss (1970)—a study of the blood donation system in the UK. Blood is donated, not sold. For society it offers the chance to establish or strengthen the altruistic tendency—a selfless giving when another's need is recognized. Sometimes children just need the presence of an adult—to be there or even simply nearby in a positive way, not necessarily to do anything actively. You will doubtless know that the word "therapeutic" in the original Greek meant being attendant on someone, a servant to another in need, before it meant treating or even curing. So in our society we can stand by with purpose, and not just be hopeless bystanders. We can try to help shift the antisocial tendency to the "altruistic social tendency".

Now the use of self flows from this perspective. Increased altruism won't happen if we don't step up our adult social exchanges with young people in our communities. Our passage through the community can present us with the equivalent of what Adrian Ward elsewhere calls "opportunity led work" (2002, pp. 111–124). Noticing and seizing the moment of opportunity to make a difference as the living day unfolds is the essence of the orientation and activity, not simply waiting until the "conflagration" takes hold. In "The Antisocial Tendency", Winnicott observes how often "one sees the moment of hope [in the child and for society too] wasted" (1956, p. 309), and it withers because of intolerance. His treatment advice is the same: go to meet and match the person's hope (that is, help make them good citizens).

So good residential work, suitably adapted, can give us a public steer towards social inclusiveness and towards a thoughtful tolerance. Winnicott saw this too and saw why it was possible to make a difference by the way that we *treat* others. His last lecture before his death in January 1971 was his 1970 David Wills lecture—"Residential care as therapy". He began by framing such work as "a kind of loving". What I call his "Pillars" to this work are highlighted in his paper:

• Reliability
• Holding
• Non-Moralistic Attitude
• No Gratitude Necessary

And flowing through and across all four pillars are communication—spaces and times, and time to talk—and an atmosphere of tolerance.

Regarding *Reliability* at the level of society, Winnicott stresses that the world young people encounter must—to a good-enough degree—be less unpredictable and powerfully confusing and more humanely approachable and habitable. In this way children can be less restless, but not fear that they must be fully compliant and conformist in order to be "acceptable" and to "matter".

As for *Holding*, and translated from the level of the personal to the level of society, when children and young people feel or fear that their emotional security has been or will be fractured, lost or attenuated, only to discover that society is indeed strong enough (if perhaps just strong enough) to offer a social level of good-enough holding—then they will feel hope, and will at least begin to believe that even if they proceed to act-up it will be recognized, named, challenged, and contained before tragedy or social catastrophe breaks out. They will not simply be overwhelmingly quashed.

Non-Moralistic Attitude—well, yes, presenting a moral attitude is important—so long as we understand it as taking notice of the actual or potential impact of people's words and actions on others and the responsibility of the person (as "I AM"—author, agent) for that impact. It is not a "moralizing from the high ground of righteousness". While I don't think that Winnicott himself would have favoured formal punishment as an end in itself, I believe he could see a positive purpose in its use so long as it made sense to everyone, including the recipient, and was measured, with an outcome very different from the imposition of a shaming vindictiveness or the triumph of a harsh intolerance.

In this respect I share Olive Stevenson's view, expressed in an earlier lecture, that Winnicott might have aligned himself with the "socialist" theologian philosopher, Paul Tillich, who had written during World War II, *Love, Power and Justice* (1960). Tillich proposed a creative justice over the common use of proportional justice. In the latter there is a detached, instrumental approach based on fixed rules and entitlement, aimed at retribution—"the punishment must fit the crime". In the former it is through a humane involvement of all that judgements are not constrained by rules alone, but are measured according to what would recognize the degree of hurt or harm done, establish restitution, and keep people safe. He called it "the form of reuniting love" (p. 66). For Winnicott, too, I believe, love enters into our understanding and approach as well as hope.

When he first encountered the possibilities of such residential treatment being put into practice was the moment, Winnicott claimed, when he began to "grow downwards" (1970, p. 220) and to feel less important himself and more respectful of the healing powers of people being actively engaged together in/as a living community. It is not hard to see the transfer of this important realization about the use of a group as a group from a bespoke community to our own wider community.

In a sufficiently well-adapted society with a strong enough democratic tendency, *No Gratitude* will ever be required, demanded, or expected. "You young kids today should be grateful; when I was ..." Even if there are some truths to these grumpy views, it is not *true*. We in our youth were facing real challenges just as they are now in theirs; if ours related to scarcity, theirs often relate to abundance, of particular kinds. (And our society has proven itself better at managing the former than the latter.) Recognition and acceptance as a member of society is not conditional. This truth holds even when some young members are for a time showing their value to it by being a nuisance and thus preventing us from becoming too complacent and satisfied with how things are. In fact even when being a nuisance on occasion most young people will continue on their journey towards becoming mature individuals capable of making a positive contribution to the common social good. Or at least this can be the case so long as when setting limits we respond to them in a human and humane way and not simply seek to crush their spirit.

So we can, I hope, see the relevance for our social way forward with the antisocial tendency—of children and even more of our adult society—when we transfer the substance, and not necessarily the form, of his ideas about residential treatment to social living, learning, and growing, and to the full integration of children and young people into our social world. There is still time for mending, which Winnicott never saw as always getting it right, but as trying, and not letting down or dropping those struggling to belong.

Towards integration

There is one other way for me of understanding and giving this social recognition and effort a boost amongst all us X, Y, and DMT people (and perhaps even Z). In the last few years, just as schools were about to reopen at the beginning of a new academic year, two items have appeared in the news. One, often voiced by politicians, expresses concerns about dissolute youth and broken societies. Arguments have run along the well-trodden lines of: "It is broken"—"It isn't broken"—"It is"—"No, it's not"—"Yes, it is"—"No, no, no ..."—"Yes, yes, yes". The other item has focused on reports about the low and still declining levels of inoculation in Britain. The concern here is that below a point when at least 90% of the population are inoculated against dangerous infectious diseases children become highly vulnerable. Currently in both France and Britain there is a major measles epidemic as both nations have inoculation levels that have fallen well below 90%. The argument runs that we need a deep pool of protection for resistance against all such dangerous bacteria or virus to work effectively. Without that, not only are non-inoculated children at risk, even inoculated ones are. It is the pool, not the individual inoculation, which protects.

Here then is the connection with the "broken society" debate as I see it. The point is similar to the one that Winnicott made about the need for a sufficient proportion of mature individuals to be present in society in order for the Democratic Tendency to be reliably present. Our society isn't broken in any crude sense, despite what politicians like to claim. However, children in our society are insufficiently inoculated against the antisocial strains to which they are exposed today and remain vulnerable. In fact over recent decades the risk they face has grown greater as the pool of inoculation against these "social diseases" has become smaller and shallower. They need a full social campaign of inoculation just as we have had against childhood killer diseases. After all Winnicott (1962) himself declared we should no longer accept the vulnerability of children to emotional illness any more than we should accept with resignation their vulnerability to poliomyelitis (polio). The inoculation all our children need to have from us alongside the MMR (measles, mumps, and rubella) vaccine is what I call the "BHL jab"—B for our fundamental Belief *in them*; H for our Hope *for them* as they might struggle themselves to hold it if not inoculated; and L for loving care *of them*.

It may sound a big challenge, but look at what we do when a global economic crisis hits—all hands to the deck for a solution. We make choices. I propose attending to this critical moment and opportunity for B, H, and L to be supplied. And the task isn't really as daunting as it might appear. Being "good enough", in Winnicott's phrase, is what is required of us.

Summing it up and holding the hope

Vaclav Havel, the former Charter 77 dissident who stood out against Soviet tyranny to become President first of liberated Czechoslovakia, and subsequently of the Czech Republic, set out what hope is and means today:

Either we have Hope within us or we don't. It is a dimension of the soul and is not essentially dependent on some particular observation of the world. It is an orientation of the spirit, an orientation of the heart. It transcends the world that is immediately experienced and is anchored somewhere beyond its horizons.

Hope in this deep and powerful sense is not the same as joy that things are going well or willingness to invest in enterprises that are obviously headed for early success. Rather it is an ability to work for something because it is good, not just because it stands a chance to succeed.

Hope is definitely not the same as optimism. It is not the conviction that something will turn out well, but the certainty that something makes sense regardless of how it turns out. It is hope, above all, which gives the strength to live and continually try new things.

(Havel, 1991, p. 181)

I hold this hope that society can become more attentive towards Winnicott's words and better attuned to providing wise care for our children and young people, so that we change direction now and try to wander less off course in the future.

References

Davies, R. (1970). *The Fifth Business. London*: Penguin Books.
Davies, R. (1972). *The Manticore*. London: Penguin Books.
Department of Health and The Home Office (2003). *The Victoria Climbié Inquiry, Report of an Inquiry by Lord Laming*, Cm 5730, January.
Füredi, F. (2003). *Therapy Culture: Cultivating Vulnerability in an Uncertain Age*. London: Routledge.
Guardian (2010). Boys, 10, 11, found guilty of attempted rape of girl, eight. 25 May.
Havel, V. (1991). *Disturbing the Peace: A Conversation with Karel Huizdala*. New York: Vantage Books.
Home Office (2010). *Crime in England and Wales: Quarterly Update to June 2010*. Available online at: www.gov.rds
Main, T. (1989). *The Ailment and Other Psychoanalytic Essays*. London: Free Association Books.
McLeod, G. (2010). Understanding obstacles to a multidisciplinary understanding of "disruptive" behaviour. *Emotional and Behavioural Difficulties*, 15(2): 95–109.

Morrison, B. (1997). *As If*. London: Granta.

Nicholls, P. (2009). A good childhood. In: R. Layard & J. Dunn (Eds.), *A Good Childhood: Searching for Values in a Competitive Age* (pp. 151–162). London: Penguin Books.

Sacks, O. (1976). *Awakenings*. London: Penguin Books.

Tillich, P. (1960). *Love, Power and Justice: Ontological Analyses and Ethical Applications*. Oxford: Oxford University Press.

Titmuss, R. (1970). *The Gift Relationship*. London: New Press.

Visser, J. & Jehan, Z. (2009). ADHD: A scientific fact or factual opinion? *Emotional and Behavioural Difficulties*, 14(2): 127–140.

Ward, A. (2002). Opportunity led work. *Therapeutic Communities*, 23(2): 111–124.

Winnicott, C. (1984). Introduction. In: C. Winnicott, R. Shepherd & M. Davies (Eds.), *Deprivation and Delinquency* (pp. 1–5). London: Tavistock Publications.

Winnicott, D. W. (1950). Some thoughts about the meaning of the word democracy. In: C. Winnicott, R. Shepherd & M. Davis (Eds.), *Home is Where We Start From* (pp. 239–259). London: Penguin.

Winnicott, D. W. (1956). The Antisocial Tendency. In: C. Winnicott, R. Shepherd & M. Davies (Eds.), *Deprivation and Delinquency*. London: Routledge, 1990.

Winnicott, D. W. (1962). Ego-integration in emotional development. In: *The Maturational Processes and the Facilitating Environment* (pp. 56–63). London: Hogarth Press, 1965.

Winnicott, D. W. (1963). Struggling through the doldrums. In: C. Winnicott, R. Shepherd & M. Davies (Eds.), *Deprivation and Delinquency* (pp. 145–155). London: Routledge, 1990.

Winnicott, D. W. (1967). Delinquency as a sign of hope. In: C. Winnicott, R. Shepherd & M. Davies (Eds.), *Home is Where We Start From* (pp. 90–100). London: Penguin, 1990.

Winnicott, D. W. (1970). Residential care as therapy. In: C. Winnicott, R. Shepherd & M. Davies (Eds.), *Deprivation and Delinquency* (pp. 220–228). London: Routledge, 1990.

Woolf, Rt Hon Lord Chief Justice & Tumin, His Honour Judge S. (1991). *Prison Disturbances in April 1990: Report of an Inquiry*. London: HMSO.

The "English riots" as a communication: Winnicott, the antisocial tendency, and public disorder

Adrian Ward

In the middle of the summer of 2011, an extraordinary whirlwind of public disorder swept briefly through London and a number of other English towns and cities. These 'riots' were apparently triggered by conflict in Tottenham between police and the friends and relatives of a young man who had been shot dead by police, although many questions were left unanswered as to what else may have contributed to the rapid rise and fall of this disorder, either in terms of broader social and political discontent, or in terms of the psychology of crowd and individual behaviour.

In this postscript to the lecture series I want to promote debate about the extent to which these 'English riots' may have been an expression of the antisocial tendency, and the extent to which they may have expressed other aspects of societal anxiety about order and disorder.

If we accept Winnicott's argument that every child is likely to show signs of the antisocial tendency as part of their innate need to test the boundaries of their environment, we can perhaps envisage the dilemmas of public order and disorder at least partly in terms of the task of the holding environment. In these terms we can read some of the spontaneous wild behaviour of young people and others on the street as equivalent to the young child's need to try out his "power to disrupt, to destroy, to frighten, to wear down, to waste, to wangle and to appropriate" (Winnicott, 1984, p. 115). If such bids for power (in children) are handled too harshly or in a spirit of retaliation they may either be temporarily suppressed or they may escalate into something more damaging—and likewise on the street—while if they are treated too leniently or with too *little* concern, they may also escalate (in either context, the family or the social). The point is for there to be a healthy and if necessary conflictual engagement, in which the strong feelings on both sides are expressed and perhaps acted out, but which can then often lead to some resolution through the renegotiation of relationships. The child expressing antisocial behaviour is seen as unconsciously seeking a suitably containing response which will recognize their growing potency but will also provide the next appropriate level of response and containment.

As we have seen, however, where the antisocial tendency is not effectively engaged with, there are real dangers of escalation, although in the "on the streets" scenario, such escalation may quickly find expression through more distorted means, in which the behaviour may seem to become less focused and more "meaningless", and because effective communication has broken down, it may well emerge in the form of serious violence and destruction.

It is through this lens of how to respond adaptively to the antisocial tendency that we will now attempt to read the "riots". It is a lens which encourages us to always look for the need behind the behaviour, for the communication hidden within the act.

Social or antisocial rioting

When we apply this approach to the recent riots, a number of questions arise.

- *First, is rioting antisocial?*

It is certainly seen as such when groups go wild and ransack their neighbourhoods; this is 'antisocial' in the sense that it is experienced by society as a direct attack, and it is clear that most of the communities affected by the 2011 riots experienced them as profoundly antisocial in that they seemed to challenge and subvert many of the commonly accepted social values in these communities. Such behaviour is not necessarily antisocial in Winnicott's sense, however, unless we have evidence that individuals are motivated in part by an unconscious wish for containment and a creative response. If we are to be clearer, we need to understand more about crowds and mobs and how they behave.

It is likely that within a large unruly crowd there will be a variety of subgroups of shifting composition and diverse motivations, and expressing a range of emotions (Waddington, 1992). Some participants may be taking (or attempting to take) a lead, perhaps implicitly "crying havoc", which was the signal given to the military in the Middle Ages to direct troops to "pillage and chaos". Others in turn may be following such a lead, although research seems to indicate that "leadership" in these situations may be extremely fluid, and very different from the media's fantasy of identifiable and powerful "ring-leaders" egging the crowd on from the side-lines. Other participants still will be further out on the fringes, excited by the mayhem and perhaps greedy for the spoils though maybe not actively looting or burning. This last group may be engaged in what has been called "recreational rioting" (e.g., Jarman et al., 2001), but I would suggest that it is within this group that we will find those letting rip with their antisocial tendency: pushing hard at the limits, while maybe unconsciously hoping for those limits to be re-established so that they can actually feel safe again. They are perhaps wanting to be stopped, although not necessarily to be caught.

In the English riots it is evident from the later charges that the ripples spread out even further, beyond those actively participating, as some were charged with receiving looted items (in some cases supposedly unwittingly) although they were not present at the events themselves.

- *Second, how do we connect—and distinguish between—individual "disorders" and public "disorder"?*

We cannot easily assume that each individual makes a conscious or rational decision as to their level of involvement. Levels of emotion run very high and change very quickly in these situations, and people may move in and out of "trouble" rapidly. Early but influential theories of crowd behaviour in terms of "contagion" (e.g., Le Bon, 1891) suggested that individuals tend to subsume or even lose their identity into the mass of the crowd, although more recent views (e.g., Reicher, 1984; Reicher et al., 2004) suggest more of a process of identification and re-identification into emergent and shifting groupings, through which people find what they believe to be their place in the crowd—although this may not remain a fixed place for long, because "the crowd" is not a fixed quantity or in a fixed location.

Trouble attracts the troubled, however, and public disorder will hold a magnetic power for some of those who feel disordered on the inside. It is hardly surprising that when disarray and destruction breaks out on the streets, some people will identify readily with the unfolding chaos and may even feel that their "moment has come", and that at last they have the opportunity to express in a public setting whatever their private distress and disturbance, or wish for containment, may be. Moreover, because others appear to be doing the same, these individuals may imagine that they can express their feelings with impunity—perhaps because they now see themselves as "the group" rather than as solo individuals, and thus (at a fantasy level) immune from detection or prosecution. The wearing of hoodies seems to feed straight into this fantasy—combining the effect of anonymity and uniformity with the imagined power of the magic cloak of invisibility.

Far from being the agitators and trouble-makers, however, these storm-followers may be the most vulnerable of all, because their hold on the rational and the individual self may be much less secure than others. They may be the most prone to getting "carried away" by the excitement, and indeed to being tipped over into greater personal distress. (We do not yet know whether levels of psychiatric referrals changed in the immediate aftermath of the riots.)

- *This leads us to our third question: Why do some episodes of community anger become disorder and then turn to riot while other occasions do not?*

We have already seen that there are sub-groups and interactive processes *within* the crowd or group and now we can consider interactions *between* the members of the crowd on the one hand and the police and other public bodies (including the media) on the other. There are few inevitable riots and probably few inevitably peaceful protests.

As policing of public disorder has developed in recent years, more account has been taken of the fact that mobs and rioting crowds are rarely monolithic or static, and that they therefore need intelligent and tactical policing if they are to be effectively contained and managed. However, it appears that in the London riots in particular, the approach taken by the police on the first two nights was perceived by many as being too disengaged, and was felt by the rioters as unrestricting, which may have contributed to rapid escalation. On other recent occasions the Metropolitan police had been criticized for being *over*-containing, especially in the use of "kettling", in which an unruly crowd is aggressively penned into a tight physical space—often for many hours and indeed sometimes illegally so, as a high court judgement only four months earlier had found (*Guardian*, 2011). By the third and fourth nights, police tactics in London changed completely, as we shall see, and order was quickly and effectively restored.

It is likely, then, that our best understanding of the riots themselves will come from looking at the interactions both within and between the various groupings involved, especially the groups and sub-groups of rioters, and the police and related authority groups. With these questions and observations in mind, we will now briefly consider the story of the English riots.

London, August 2011

On 6 August, two days after the police shooting of Mark Duggan, a young black man in North London, a (largely female) group of his friends and family gathered outside Tottenham police station to seek answers. They were following a well-established procedure in that area for communication between police and the community in times of high tension, and they were supported by community representatives.

However, this situation seems to have been handled clumsily and with great anxiety by the senior officer on duty, so that after several hours those asking the questions had obtained no answers, communication had broken down, and the group came away frustrated and angry. These feelings soon spread to others in the immediate neighbourhood and within two hours had escalated into anger and violence: two police cars were set alight, and later a bus was burned. Shops were looted, TV crews attacked, fires were started. News spread quickly across the borough by word of mouth and by social networking and other media. Episodes of unrestrained looting and arson continued throughout that night across the borough.

The following night there was similar trouble in the neighbouring borough of Enfield and then in Brixton and Hackney, with more fires and looting. There was increasing alarm in the community that things were getting out of hand, and that the police had appeared unable or even unwilling to intervene. On the third night the destruction spread outwards to Croydon with a very serious fire, but also to Birmingham and elsewhere in England—although not to Scotland or Wales. By the fourth night—10/11 August—the last of these troubles had erupted but had also been contained.

Police tactics changed markedly from an initial state of apparent unreadiness, helplessness, and even retreat, into a far more containing response with much greater numbers and more assertive action, although largely (apparently) without indulging in the sort of violent counter-attack including water-cannon, baton rounds, and even live ammunition which was already being called for in parts of the media and by some politicians.

By now these short-lived English riots had first erupted and had then either been subdued or had exhausted themselves. The aftermath of the riots lasted much longer than the riots themselves, which began and ended within four nights. Even though the violence on the streets sub-sided relatively quickly, the repercussions for those brought to court were extreme, with some reports suggesting that sentences were far heavier for these offences than for equivalent crimes at other times, under clear instruc-tion from government. Repercussions for the victims were also great, with many people losing accommodation, possessions, and livelihoods.

I must emphasize that I did not personally witness any of the disor-der taking place, although I was in Ealing shortly afterwards and saw not only the signs of damage but the cards and bunches of flowers left at the spot where a man died after trying to intervene to prevent further violence. I have full sympathy for those terrified and even bereaved by the effects of these riots.

Perspectives on the riots

So what were the riots about? How do we explain the sudden pande-monium ("the loosing of all the devils"), with gangs of people emerging apparently from nowhere, ransacking, looting, burning, and running wild, some of them apparently oblivious to the risk of being identified and caught? Were the riots in Tottenham the same as those in Ealing or in Manchester? Why did they not spread to Glasgow or Bridgend? Why did they stop again so suddenly?

There have been many suggestions as to what was going on. Some observers were only surprised at the fact that it had taken so long to explode, having anticipated that the rapidly worsening economic climate over the previous two or three years would lead to social unrest (as in Greece) once its impact was felt more broadly in terms of increased unemployment, poverty, and consequent despair.

Some of the comment was to the effect that these were riots of envy or greed, rather than "real riots" or, in other words, political riots, focused on a "cause" or demand, or stemming from immediate need such as the food riots experienced in Gujarat in 2002 (Samudhay, 2002). In this scenario the looting was viewed as an orgy of consumerist excitement, an unauthorized version of "supermarket sweep", no holds barred. Some, on the other hand, did see the riots as indirectly political in their mirroring of the greed and lawlessness of bankers or of politicians and even the police themselves, on the basis that if those powerful people can "get away with it" then so can we. This view found unexpected sympathy in a *Daily Mail* editorial:

> [T]he bankers have the same contempt for the law-abiding public as those looters and the same sense of entitlement to wealth as the teenagers who smash shop windows to steal flat-screen televisions.

> (*Daily Mail*, 2011)

There is probably something in each of these views, although I also think other factors were at play. My suggestion is that for many of the rioters this was "acting out" on a grand scale—the unthought-out actions of delinquent excitement in which people had become temporarily caught up in wild and illegal behaviour. There will undoubtedly have been agitators and opportunists as there are in all such situations, and probably an instant network of illegal traders for those wanting to dispose of high-value looted items for quick cash. But a good proportion of the young people out on the streets will have been whipped along into the whirlwind, perhaps briefly sensing a distorted feeling of power and agency which they may never have experienced before, and finding that, for a few brief hours, there was almost nothing or no-one to restrain them.

One group of girls interviewed in passing on the street on the second night said things like: "We're just showing the police we can do what we like" and "We're going to keep on rioting till someone stops us"—as well as "it's payback time" and "it's our turn now". This is where it starts to sound like Winnicott's antisocial tendency, the combination of resentful act and hopeful gesture, but also the wish to be caught or at least stopped—and I will return to that theme later.

What was also noticeable was the polarizing effect of the riots in society and especially among young people themselves, with many of them extremely angry and distressed about what was happening, while others felt more sympathy and looked for more explanation. There was much demonizing of young people, and of teenagers in particular, as well as of their parents, and the word "feral" was used frequently, often uttered with spitting contempt. Such language has the effect of conveying both disgust and rejection and the wish to distance oneself from the problem. The printed and broadcast media became extremely excited, with many live broadcasts from the scenes around the capital in particular. Many conclusions were jumped to, especially that the rioters were primarily gangs of teenagers, although even the Home Secretary soon had to revise that assumption—relatively few of those arrested seem to have been gang members (Ministry of Justice, 2011).

In fact it probably never made sense to see this as gang-related behaviour—in most places it was far too impulsive and random for that. It seems more likely that the riots arose within groups rather than gangs—*large* groups, the instant groupings in which crowds gather together in a moment, turn into mobs, and renounce individual conscience for immediate gratification. Levels of anxiety within the rioting groups appeared to be extremely high, with both fight and flight operating simultaneously. It is very difficult to speculate as to what may have been going on in each of the individuals who made up these groups to make them so ready to riot, but we do need to try to explain it. We have already seen how the questions of the patterns of interaction both within and between the various groupings, including the police, may have affected the course of events. It may also be helpful to draw upon some of our professional experience of working with antisocial and troubled youth.

Working with adolescent disorder

My own early social work experience was in working with extremely troubled young people in residential settings and trying to help them understand themselves and take control of themselves and their lives so that they could (as Melvyn Rose memorably expressed it) "convert their thoughtless acts into act-less thoughts" (verbal communication)—in other words, so that they would be less prone to destructive or violent behaviour and more able to express themselves effectively.

One of the most useful pieces of theory which I drew upon in those days was Barbara Dockar-Drysdale's view that violence is nearly always the result of a breakdown in communication (Dockar-Drysdale, 1971, p. 123)—it was very rarely completely mindless, even though it might often be unconsciously driven. If it was truly mindless you needed to be very worried and take serious action. In the great majority of cases, however, even what appeared to be mindless and sometimes vicious violence turned out to have indeed been triggered by some breakdown, of communication, of understanding, or of relationship. Once the nature and cause of this breakdown was identified and understood and, where possible, resolved, the need for further violence usually disappeared. Ideally there could also be learning from the situation so that the next time a similar breakdown occurred, the young person could speak rather than fight. To restore order we would first have to restore some form of communication.

What this approach calls for in those working with these young people is the ability to see beyond the behaviour and try to understand the need behind it, and to persist in helping the young person to identify and explain the sense of wrong, or pain, or impingement, which they had experienced, but which they had not been able to recognize or articulate. The most challenging part of this work was often to identify exactly what was the communication which had broken down and how or why it had happened. Sometimes the breakdown will have consisted of the absence of a wished-for response to a verbal initiative on the part of the young person, or perhaps disappointment over a long-awaited parental visit which was cancelled or just didn't happen. Sometimes it would be at a much more hidden or symbolic level, although there was still something of a sense of grievance, or absence, or other breakdown—leading to feelings of hurt and impotent rage and then to actions including violent attack, all escalating extremely rapidly.

When all this happens in a regulated planned environment like a therapeutic community it is hard enough—but when it happens free-range, in the open environment of life on the estate or on the high street, it is much harder to deal with. Likewise when it happens within one individual it may be possible to respond and contain the rage—whereas when it happens within fluid and evolving groupings it is much harder to do so effectively.

In fact the people of Broadwater Farm where Mark Duggan lived had more experience than most of learning from the pain of violence and disorder. Following the Tottenham riots in 1985 there seem to have evolved effective liaison groups and youth leadership, and well-established ways of handling breakdowns when they happened. It appears that these semi-formal procedures of consultation between police and trusted community members had led to a relatively peaceful co-existence. Unfortunately on 6 August 2011 this collaboration was disrupted, probably because of anxiety, and communication clearly broke down, so that the initial delegation of family and friends came away hopeless and furious—and the scene was set for that same rapid escalation.

One of the most de-stabilizing aspects of that first night was the apparent lack of an effective policing response. The job of police in such situations is primarily to keep order: to prevent disorder, to restore order, and to contain and then dispel the explosive atmosphere on the streets. On that first night in Tottenham they seem to have been unable to do so, or to have lacked the confidence or will to do so. In this context it is worth remembering that only two weeks earlier the Metropolitan Police Commissioner had resigned with immediate effect in connection with the phone-hacking scandal and allegations of police corruption, so the police may have had good reason to feel directionless and uncontained themselves.

For whatever reason, the riots—and especially the mass looting—in Tottenham that night were largely uncontained. The controls were off, and the crowds in the streets quickly slipped the leash of the law and raced through selected stores, breaking and taking. It may perhaps have been these repeated images of unharnessed looting which then excited those elsewhere to have the confidence to take similar risks on the following nights, and which led those girls to talk about looting "until someone stopped them". It was an invitation to go large on the antisocial tendency.

Stopping them, of course, is exactly what did happen. On the third and fourth nights, national policing resources were co-ordinated so that much greater numbers could be deployed in the key areas. Controls were re-imposed, the boundaries re-established, and the circle of expectation that each night would bring further disorder was broken. This is a very familiar pattern for those with experience of residential care for adolescents: on some occasions you have to be made to experience the very worst, and to fear and even expect further deterioration, before you can find the real resolve and ability to de-escalate and restore order, both external and internal—to establish peace of mind as well as calm on the streets. By the fifth and sixth nights after the riots had started, although community anxiety was still very high in some areas, there was almost no trouble, and no real expectation that there would be. What was left was some serious clearing up and self-examination all round, and an awful sense that society had temporarily exploded to reveal its capacity for destruction—but also for re-creation and in some cases for vengeful justice.

There has been some debate as to whether these riots were "proper riots" or just "mindless violence", as if "mind*ful* violence" would some-how have been preferable. It is very hard to know in what sense any of these rioters and looters may have been expressing political anger rather than collective delinquency, but there may be another way of looking at the passions which were driving these activities. I am sug-gesting that there is unconscious political anger—varying from rage against the machine to the outpouring of frustration at relentless tedium and meaninglessness, although we are still left with the question: "Why now?"

The effects of the riots

Finally we can return to the question: In what sense were these riots social or antisocial? A different way to answer this question is to turn our attention away from the intention of the rioters and to look instead at the impact and outcome of the riots. While there was undoubtedly a broad public reaction of horror and anger at the destructiveness, and demands for justice, there was also a sense of these riots having been a "wake-up call", a reminder that when there is increased poverty and despair there is always the potential for serious disturbance motivated by anger, and as we have seen, the parallels with the apparent antisocial behaviour of bankers, MPs, and police were widely remarked. There was increased recognition that some young people had indeed been affected powerfully by the economic difficulties facing the country. The effects of the riots might therefore be argued to be social rather than antisocial, and even to be *pro*-social in the sense of reminding us all that there *is* such a thing as society, and that it includes many very disadvan-taged and deprived people.

At the same time, it cannot be denied that there was also a great deal of delinquency on the nights of the riots. But delinquency, in Winnicott's view, can also be seen as a sign of hope—because it suggests that it is *worth* being delinquent, worth pushing the boundaries, that "I am important enough to be able to act and exert power". This hope will only be realized if the underlying communication is heard, however.

Delinquency also brings excitement and thus secondary gain which usually brings more risk. Dockar-Drysdale (1961, p. 171) also wrote about "converting delinquent excitement into oral greed" (or possibly converting it *back* into oral greed). In disorder in adolescent institutions the sooner you could find a way to provide food or warm drink in a form in which it could be accepted and gulped down, the sooner you could restore order. I don't know how you could manage that in a street riot, but soup kitchens down side-streets might not be a bad idea. In fact what was most important in residential care was, through the use of food, to restore a nurturing relationship by means of which the young people could feel genuinely cared for at a personal level, and this is what may turn out to be the task facing us all in relation to the more troubled young people of our generation: to care more fully both for and about them.

References

Daily Mail (2011). Comment Column: Bankers, looters and the politics of envy. 11 August. Available online at: www.dailymail.co.uk/debate/

Dockar-Drysdale, B. F. (1961). Making adaptations to the needs of the individual child in a group. In: *The Provision of Primary Experience* (pp. 167–177). London: Free Association Books.

Dockar-Drysdale, B. F. (1971). Problems in the management of violence in disturbed children. In: *Therapy and Consultation in Child Care* (pp. 123–136). London: Free Association Books.

Guardian (2011). Kettling of G20 protesters by police was illegal, high court rules. 14 April. Available online at: www.guardian.co.uk/uk/2011/apr/14/kettling-g20-protesters-police-illegal

Jarman, N. & O'Halloran, C. (2011). Recreational rioting: Young people, interface areas and violence. *Child Care in Practice, 7(1)*: 2–16.

Le Bon, G. (1895/1947). *The Crowd: A Study of the Popular Mind*. London: Ernest Benn.

Ministry of Justice (2011). *Statistical Bulletin on the Public Disorder of 6th to 9th August 2011—October Update*.

Reicher, S. D. (1984). The St. Pauls' riot: An explanation of the limits of crowd action in terms of a social identity model. *European Journal of Social Psychology, 14*: 1–21.

Reicher, S., Stott, C., Cronin, P. & Otto Adang, O. (2004). An integrated approach to crowd psychology and public order policing. *Policing: An International Journal of Police Strategies & Management, 27(4)*: 558–572.

Samudhay, A, (2002). *Riots: Psychosocial Care by Community Level Helpers for Survivors*. Bangalore: Books for Change.

Waddington, D. (1992). *Contemporary Issues in Public Disorder*. London: Routledge.

Winnicott, D. W. (1984). Some psychological aspects of juvenile delinquency. In: C. Winnicott, R. Shepherd & M. Davis (Eds.), *Deprivation and Delinquency* (pp. 113–119). London: Tavistock.

For Product Safety Concerns and Information please contact our EU
representative GPSR@taylorandfrancis.com
Taylor & Francis Verlag GmbH, Kaufingerstraße 24, 80331 München, Germany

www.ingramcontent.com/pod-product-compliance
Lightning Source LLC
Chambersburg PA
CBHW052011270326
41929CB00015B/2869